The Struggles of

The Struggles of Getting an Education

Issues of Power, Culture, and Difference for Mexican Americans of the Southwest

by Barbara Sparks

Educational Studies Press
College of Education
Northern Illinois University
DeKalb, IL 60115

© 2002 by Educational Studies Press
Printed in the United States of America

Managing Editor: Donna Smith
Substantive Editor: Susan Timm
Cover Art: Director, Mary Lou Read-Dreyer; Designer, Michelle
Campbell

Distributed by Educational Studies Press

Library of Congress Catalog-in-Publication Data
Sparks, Barbara, 1948-
   Educating Chicanos in urban communities : the impact of
structural-cultural factors on
 nonparticipation in adult basic educationation / by Barbara Sparks.
      p. cm.
   Includes bibliographic references.
   ISBN 1-879528-25-8 (alk. paper)
    1. Mexican Americans—Education. 2. Mexican Americans—
   Ethnic identity. 3. Education, Urban—United States. 4. Adult
   education—United States. 5. Basic education—United States. I.
   Title.

LC2683 .S62 2001
374'.182968'72073—dc21
                                                    2001023715

Dedicated to my mother,
Honorine Vande Walle Engebos

Table of Contents

Acknowledgments

This book project is the result of several years of effort supported by a number of people without whom the finished product would have been impossible. Because of the length of the project there may be some individuals whom I have forgotten to thank and apologize if this is the case. It is not intentional.

With a background in adult literacy instruction and administration, I undertook the research questions addressed here as the focus of my doctoral study and dissertation but persisted in getting the findings published for the Chicanas and Chicanos whose stories provide testimony to the continuous educational discrimination and struggle that goes on, often unnoticed. There are few examples of adult literacy learners' perspectives about their own needs and experiences, to say nothing of the actions they engage in as they struggle to get an education. I thank each of them for allowing me to share their views and recognize that if they had written this book the emphasis may have been different. I believe it is important to hear their voices and use the information to improve and change literacy programs so that they work for learners and promote social justice.

I want to thank those who helped me get into the field and pointed me in the right direction, or occasionally led me, to the people whose stories are included in this book. They include Sharon Stone, Manuela

Nehls, Pat Montoya, Mary Monoz, Vicky Procheska, Patsy Terrones, Jossie Rodriquez, Father Bill Martinez, Martha Crawley, Sylvia Rodriquez, Elaine Bradford, Tim Galvin, Chuck Tafoya, Francis Arellano, and Tomasita Oretga.

I am grateful to Rudi Benavidez for translating documents critical to carrying out the interviews, to Reuben Martinez for his candor and insights into racial politics in the community, and to Erving Lucero for our discussions about the strength of the deeply embedded link between language and identity. Devon Pena provided inspiration and guidance which was invaluable. Major funding for the research was provided through the Colorado Department of Education with 353 funds from the U.S. Department of Education, Adult Basic Education Act. Dian Bates, then Director of the Adult Education Section in Colorado, was instrumental in securing these funds, while the Denver Indian Center acted as fiscal agent under the watchful eyes and support of Linda Nuttal and Lisa Harjo. Having the funding afforded me the opportunity to focus on the project without having to hold down a full time job that is so common among folks trying to complete a dissertation.

I want to thank my doctoral committee chaired by Larry Martin, a literacy scholar who pushed me to clarify my inquiry and analysis, who spent numerous hours discussing ideas, and who provided me with continuous support when I was in the field. He always encouraged me to reach for a critical understanding and continues to be one of my major supporters. To Dale Jaffe, I give credit for turning me into a qualitative researcher while Ian Harris often challenged me to question what I thought I knew. Jim Fisher was willing to engage me in debate and Diane Pollard provided last minute support and balance to the process. Two other scholars were especially important to my intellectual growth and development. I want to thank Jim Cibulka who not only guided me through the graduate program but critiqued my writing and facilitated my critique of many educational policy issues. Steven Haymes arrived at the Milwaukee campus as a visiting professor just when I needed him the most.

I want to thank Dan Folkman who tirelessly listened, discussed, and helped me think through and critique my ideas and my writing all along the way. His friendship was truly invaluable. Jerry Wartgow gave me that nudge out the door which sent me on the journey in the first place. I am grateful for his belief in me.

I conducted an initial pilot study in Chicago to test out some of my ideas and lines of inquiry. Without the access, support and friendship of Olivia Flores Godinez this would have been much more difficult. She engaged me in hours of discussions and introduced me to staff and adult learners at Universidad Popular and the community of Pilsen. She also introduced me to Jorge Reyes at Instituto del Progresso Latino who recruited new literacy learners to talk with me about their experiences and concerns. The information I gathered during that time provided a foundational base from which to launch the study reported here.

Donna Smith, my editor, has been especially helpful in reviewing and editing the manuscript and sticking with me throughout the publication process. Susan Timm provided editorial comments that strengthened the finished copy.

Family members always play a significant role in any effort such as this. My father and sisters were valuable backers and my deceased mother provided inspiration. Most importantly, I want to thank my children, Chad and Rachael, who were active supporters and cheerleaders at every step. We were all in college at the same time and they proved to be excellent scholars in challenging my thinking, and they also provided personal respite and humor which was essential to my journey.

Introduction

This is a story about educational struggle, the story of how working class Mexican American adults have struggled for their right to an education; a story that is missing from the adult literacy reports. It is also a story of resistance, a resistance to the unrelenting discrimination, inside and outside of schooling, that Mexican Americans have experienced because of their racial and ethnic status. Finally, this is a story of how government funded adult basic education (ABE) and English literacy programs contribute to the Mexican American struggle for educational equality. It documents the stories of thirty men and women who try to get an education in a society that seeks to assimilate them into the dominant culture because it does not accept them as they are. These men and women tell of their educational experiences that are embedded in wider historical and contemporary social, cultural, economic, and political arenas of life. They also tell of the cultural actions they took to meet their self-identified educational needs and the continuous struggles they engaged in as they did so.

My interest in this struggle grew out of my involvement in adult basic education, first as a teacher and then as an administrator in state-administrated programs for adults who wanted to learn English and other basic academic skills of reading, writing, and mathematics. I worked primarily with Mexican Americans in urban barrios, the separated enclaves, or neighborhoods, within cities where Latinos live, one in the Midwest and the others in the Southwest, and I had the opportunity, at other times, to visit and observe rural programs that served large numbers of Mexican Americans. As a state-level employee with the community college system in Colorado, who was responsible for educational outreach, I noticed the uneven access to programs in some communities with large numbers of Hispanics. I started to question why more Hispanics were not enrolled in adult education programs. This initial question formed the basis of my doctoral research several years later (Sparks 1995). Through my work as a literacy provider and during research interviews, I witnessed the obstacles Mexican Americans face, their desire to learn, and the hope they hold in the educational process while at the same time recognizing the social and economic limitations placed on them. I undertook this study to gain a deeper understanding of the challenges they face and how they contend with the challenges.

The questions I raised about educational struggle were embedded in traditional adult education literature of participation and nonparticipation. Searching this tradition led me to investigate cultural differences, social systems, and values. Taking a very short walk through the adult education participation literature foreshadowed my concerns about the Mexican Americans I have gotten to know through programs and this study. This was my journey.

Some Perspectives on Personal Barriers

Nonparticipation in traditional adult basic education programs remains a major concern for educational practitioners and administrators because of the small number of eligible adults who actually engage in programs. Just under 6 percent of the ninety million people eligible for services participate (National Center for Education Statistics 1993). Several faulty beliefs or myths continue to be used, however, to explain issues of nonparticipation. First, there is the assumption that while obstacles exist, they can be overcome. Second, once these barriers, such as time, cost, and location are removed, people will engage in traditional programs. Third, if people do not engage in mainstream programs once the barriers are removed, it is their lack of motivation, a deficit, that impedes them. Some contend that while barriers to engagement in learning opportunities exist, these obstacles are not insurmountable. This is a privileged view of choice masking the social, economic, and political forces that intercede in motivation and desire. The majority of the studies on issues of participation have been conducted with Anglo middle-class individuals enrolled in various types of adult education and professional development training, and are of limited value when applied to groups outside the mainstream, particularly Mexican Americans and other people of color, women, and members of lower economic status.

Investigating the failure of adults to engage in adult basic education, Beder (1990) assumed that at least three reasons explain why adults do not attend programs. They lack sufficient motivation, they are motivated but are deterred in some way, or they are unaware that adult basic education programs exist. (Yet, a National Center for Education Statistics study released in 1997 states that over a third of the 94 percent of nonparticipating adults knew about adult basic education programs, suggesting there are other reasons for not enrolling in these programs.) Based on assumptions of low motivation, motivated but deterred in some way, or lack of awareness, Beder found that adults elect not to participate for a variety of situational reasons such as enrollment difficulties or a dislike for school, in other words, for reasons primarily attributed to attitudes or perceptions about adult basic education. Beder notes "it is quite possible that nonparticipators' negative attitudes and perceptions pertain to school itself rather than to the more general concept of [English] literacy" (217).

Lack of motivation studies focus on notions of individual orientations to learning such as a low perception of need for academic training because one is too old or because one's economic situation does not require certain basic skills. Included in this line of thinking is the idea that some cultures do not value education as highly as the dominant middle class. This belief that is commonly held by the mainstream culture also assumes academically underskilled people do not know, for example, that their oral English skills are weak or that they need assistance in reading or computing mathematics and, thus, by implication, their cultural background and values or lack of sophistication preclude them from knowing their true needs. These learning orientations and attitudes of self are considered dispositional barriers (Cross 1981; Darkenwald and Merriam 1982). Lack of motivation supposedly focuses on one's desire to learn, but it also suggests that people voluntarily participate (or not) in educational programs, implying a choice.

In attempting to predict continuing education participation, Scanlan and Darkenwald (1984) found that the barriers perspective and the motivation orientation was too simplistic; rather a multidimensional construct of deterrent factors proved to be a more significant predictor of participation and nonparticipation. By this it is meant that there are multiple aspects to the deterring factors. For example, situational barriers are not simply one's work situation, but also involve individual motivation regarding the desire for promotion and attitudes toward the worth of the learning encounter. The single most influential factor, consisting of many individually discreet items, centers mainly on a person's perceptions about one's self-discipline and orientation toward the desirability and importance of learning.

The Deterrents to Participation Scale, developed by Darkenwald and his colleagues (Darkenwald and Merriam 1982; Scanlan and Darkenwald 1984; Darkenwald and Valentine 1985), was used to explore the barriers faced by low English literate Puerto Rican adults. A survey of Puerto Ricans enrolled in English as a Second Language (ESL) program in the Northeast (Hayes 1989), found the most highly ranked barriers to seeking an education program related to lack of time, low priority of education in relation to work, costs, and lack of transportation. In the typology, the least deterred were young women who lived in the United States more than six years, who had an elementary education, and who had school-age children. The most likely deterred were those identified as noneducationally-oriented workers, with less than a fifth-grade education, who were employed and were an average age of thirty-two. Additionally, other most likely deterred groups were identified as unemployed mothers, educationally insecure homemakers, and the culturally isolated/unemployed. While these "groups of individuals" give a sense of who participates and who does not, it is less helpful in acknowledging and explaining the underlying reasons for the barriers. Even in Hayes's study of Puerto Ricans, explanations of cultural differences were overlooked.

As a whole, this line of inquiry focuses on the individual and actions taken or not taken in reference to engaging in adult education. Such a psychological perspective attempts to discover the internal motivators and external environmental influences that contribute to, or dispose one to, learning in formal educational situations. Descriptive analysis of participating adults, profiles of individual characteristics, motivational studies investigating orientations to learning, and identification of barriers to participating have provided a wealth of information on individual involvement in adult education. However, this psychological perspective also suggests that nonparticipating individuals are deficient somehow, and that they don't fit with Eurocentric values of individual competition and motivation. The dominant discourse, as one discourse of motivation, implies a choice, an act of will, which contributes to the individuality of the learning activity. The ideology of choice moves the blame onto those who are judged to be "illiterate" on the basis that they could have chosen otherwise.

Individualizing Social Problems

There are other risks of approaching participation as a problem in motivation such as "reifying motivation at the expense of situational factors that also bear a heavy influence upon the event of participation. The event of participation is looked at as though it were an isolated act in the person's life, rather than as an integral part of the person's life situation and social context" (Rockhill 1983, 23). Individual lives cannot be compartmentalized where schooling and education are viewed as disconnected to the whole of people's daily experiences. For example, economic necessity of holding down multiple jobs in order to care for one's family makes it virtually impossible to add educational classes to daily life, often no matter how much one may desire to do so. Poverty is an integral part of many lives and predominates the majority of those eligible for adult basic education and English literacy programs. Poverty is a social problem that ends up being heaved onto the shoulders of those individuals who carry the burden.

Compounded barriers of cultural difference, discrimination, and racism also define the social context of daily life for the majority of the population who do not belong to the middle class. How do such circumstances affect not only participation in adult education, but desire, opportunity, and ability? These are some of the questions this book attempts to answer. Reluctance to acknowledge the role that cultural differences, discrimination, and racism, within the larger context of society, play in adult basic education and English literacy, further compartmentalizes daily lives.

Interestingly, these collective social problems are seen as individualistic situations that make potential adult basic education and English literacy learners appear to be deficient or lacking. Deficit thinking, a prevalent viewpoint in educational circles, compares everyone to a dominant norm, and if the individual does not measure up, he or she must be fixed, or healed, as in the medical model of treatment. There is an assumption that the learner needs to be changed. In adult basic education and English literacy, this normative process is accomplished through continuous testing and retesting that identifies individual weaknesses, and through the practice of individualized instruction, seeks to allegedly address more directly those weaknesses in a time efficient manner. Cultural deficits are attributed to differences in language, ethnic values, and lifestyles that create barriers to assimilating into the dominant culture. A cultural deficit approach characterizes low-skill adult learners as lazy, unaware of their academic needs, or undisciplined, without ever considering how programs, and society in general, are complicit in causing student failure.

The struggle to successfully complete adult literacy programs also suggests there are monumental obstacles for those seeking access to socioeconomic mobility through culturally insensitive learning environments (Martin 1990). Many adult basic education and English literacy programs are administered and implemented by the white middle class using a white, middle-class curriculum and ideology. Are these culturally insensitive learning environments? Nieto (1998) suggests that teachers who deny cultural differences among learners are practicing a subtle form of tyranny. If Mexican American learners decide not to enroll in these kinds of programs, is it the motivation of the learners or of the teachers that ought to be examined?

The perception is that undereducated adults are a social burden that cost this nation billions of dollars in lost income and taxes, in addition to the money spent for welfare programs and prisons. The structures of schooling and society are protected from social criticism by focusing on remedial programs of adult basic education and English literacy. Questions as to how the practices, mechanisms, and relationships within these structures influence people's decisions and actions need to be asked.

A model of nonparticipation based on individual barriers masks the social inequalities, political struggles, and cultural differences that Mexican Americans experience. The radically different basis of oppression and subordination that such individuals contend with, and the meaning they make of those experiences, suggest a different explanation for nonparticipation in adult basic education programs. Larger societal structures beyond schooling, including capitalism, patriarchy, and racism, must also be taken into account.

Outline of Chapters

As historical subjects, people are situated within specific moments in time. Therefore, it is necessary to gain a contextualized view of the people who have participated in this project if we are to fully understand the realities they have lived. While this study looks at the realities of Mexican Americans of the Southwest, the findings can apply to Chicanos/as more broadly, and to others who have experienced various interlocking systems of colonization. The book has theoretical and practical implications for understanding culture and difference in the broader Eurocentric schooling context. The first chapter details the study itself and provides the theoretical underpinnings I used in my inquiry. Sociological constructs, including the dialectic between the individual and society, are important, as well as how hegemony manifests through adult basic education and English literacy. Focusing on the agency of Mexican American adult learners assists in examining how people respond to certain aspects of schooling and learning. Narrative profiles of five individuals whom I talked with form the next chapter, helping to personalize and make real the aggregate data. Chapter Three presents a short analysis of Mexican American colonization in the Southwest, and proceeds to show how people's identity is formed and reformed within historical and contemporary experiences. I show the connections this has to participation and nonparticipation in adult basic education. Chapter Four documents people's early educational experiences that forms another piece of the mosaic upon which subsequent decisions are made, and actions taken as people pursue educational goals. Chapter Five offers views of adult basic education programs and the experiences of those who have participated in such programs at some point in their adult lives, as well as an analysis of the similarities of their educational experiences as youth and as adults. Chapter Six provides a range of cultural actions, or practices of resistance, adults have chosen as they attempted to deal with educational and learning issues. Last, Chapter Seven provides an analysis of the dialectics of human agency and societal structures, as well as a look at specific factors that limit Chicano/a participation in adult basic education plus suggestions for restructuring programs for them and other nondominant groups.

Before moving on, however, something must be said about the terms used to describe Mexican Americans. There is no ethnic label that is unanimously regarded as the most appropriate or the most correct. Terms of self-identification used by individuals who participated in the study include Chicano/a, Spanish, and Mexican. Chicano/a refers to persons, male and female respectively, of Mexican descent, born in the United States, who align themselves with the political movement of La Raza, founded in the 1960s. It is often used interchangeably with the term Mexican American. Spanish, Spanish-origin, and Hispanic (as used in the Southwestern United States) are broader terms that refer to persons of Spanish heritage, while Latino/a refers to persons of Latin American heritage from Central America and South America, as well as Mexico (Segura 1993, 213). The term Hispanic is an English word coined by the United States Bureau of the Census to identify all Spanish-speaking and/or Spanish origin populations in the United States (de la Tore and Pesquera 1994, xiii), and is not typically used for self-identification as noted by Shorris (1992), and is supported by this study. To complicate this further, however, in some cases in northern New Mexico, Hispanic is used as a self-identifier by those privileging their Spanish heritage over their mixed Mexican, Indian, and European ancestry. For additional information on the origins and use of the term Chicano, in particular its political implications, see Barrera (1979). I will use the term Mexican American and Chicano/a interchangeably. In citing references, the term used in the original text is quoted.

Chapter 1

Adult Education as a Social Institution

> More than ever before, there is a growing realization that the established scholarship has tended to define America too narrowly (Takaki 1993, 6).

Dominant discourses of "dropout" give the appearance that those who enter adult programs but leave before completion do not want to participate or are not interested in education while ignoring the underlying problems within adult programs such as discrimination and the ideology of middle class bias that guides and maintains them. "The ideology of adult education achieves for practitioners a promise to their clientele that their primary concern will be with students' needs and interests" (Keddie 1980, 46), rather than larger societal problems such as racism and hegemonic practices. Such commitments undergird middle-class values and encourage educators and others to overlook more meaningful references based on differing cultural, social, and structural locations.

A single focus of explaining the world must give way to allow other voices, other realities to be heard; "We cannot really hear or speak about what is muted" (Lugones 1990, 49). The dearth of studies on adult basic education with Mexican Americans attests to the silence. Lugones further speaks of the "cracked mirrors" that falsely reflect Hispanic and Latino/a realities, realities that are not consistent with Anglo middle-class realities.

There is an increasing need for culturally democratic and responsive adult programs for Mexican Americans. As a young and growing population they will influence the social fabric of the future, yet a large number will be denied access to contribute fully in United States economic, political, social, and cultural life. Mexican Americans, and Latinos as a whole, are not given much attention in English literacy research nor are they provided equitable services in this country. Educationally, a number of factors contribute to this limited access to full participation in society.

The Politics of Education

Although a large majority of Hispanic adults are bilingual, there is a failure by the dominant culture to recognize Spanish literacy and its significance (Valdes 1993). This failure to recognize Spanish language abilities as literacy implies that English literacy is the only literacy that counts. The assumptive stance of such a view increases the "alleged pool of illiterates who are stigmatized as being nonproductive" (Macias 1990, 6) rather than recognizing the valuable biliteracy resources people possess. Whereas certain bilingual Anglos are valued members of society, bilingual minorities are considered conflicted and unassimilated into American culture. Native language affirms one's cultural identity as a people, while English skills indicate an attempt to acculturate into the dominant culture. There is an interest among many Hispanics in being bilingual and bicultural (Nieto 1998). Public schooling always has played a pivotal role in assimilating immigrants and other nonmainstream individuals by stripping them of their cultural identity in an effort to impose the dominant culture on them. The pressure to assimilate is evident when Spanish language is seen as a problem. As one of the largest Spanish-speaking countries, there is a need to legitimize first language (Spanish) literacy in the United States.

Hispanics face institutional constraints as they attempt to complete secondary education. Individual testimony of undereducated Hispanics almost always begins with the failure of the public schools to teach people how to read and write English. The gap between Hispanics and other Americans continues to be wide. In 2000, less that six in ten Hispanics twenty-five years of age and over had at least a high school diploma (National Council of La Raza 2001). Many narratives tell of misassessments of academic abilities and tracking into low-ability groups, as well as discriminatory discipline and promotion practices. Equally evident are the underfunded and run-down public school facilities in lower-class neighborhoods and barrios. Economic, social, and political consequences of limited reading and writing abilities among Hispanics are the same as those evidenced among other minority racial, ethnic, and gender groups. Although these consequences have not been well documented for Hispanics (Cumming 1992), limited literacy abilities, nonetheless, diminish employment opportunity, political participation, and the ability of Hispanic parents to intercede in the education of their children.

Hispanic adults who seek to enroll in English literacy or basic education programs are often turned away, placed on waiting lists, or charged for services for which they cannot pay. I saw this in multiple programs in Colorado, as well as in programs in midwestern cities of Chicago and Milwaukee, suggesting these are widespread problems that point to the historic underfunding of adult basic education and English literacy. In many urban areas, programs are limited to how many people can be served at any one time in crowded facilities commonly located in community colleges, high schools, store fronts, or church basements, and are staffed with few, if any, full-time instructors. In most rural communities, access to adult basic education and English literacy programs is equally problematic, with part-time hours of operation and often only one part-time instructor. This means that few students can be accommodated, or a small number of programs have to service multiple counties spread over many miles, making it difficult for people to get to education centers.

According to federal records of the Committee on Labor and Human Relations, the average spending per student in adult basic education is about $400. When compared to elementary and secondary per pupil expenditures of $4000 to $5000, one can see the dilemmas underfunding can create in terms of staff development and training, full-time professionals, and any other kind of quality improvement in the system. Only 25 percent of the teaching force is full-time, and there is a long history of volunteer involvement in the adult basic education system. Almost 75 percent of all programs have volunteers serving as tutors (Senate 1995, 14, 17). At the same time, however, the issue of underfunding is often used as a scapegoat for complacency toward inadequate services and low quality programs. Generally, public and private efforts to address the problems of access for Hispanics have been insufficient. Programs tend to serve those who are easiest to reach and assume some level of oral English fluency. Traditionally, Hispanics have been underserved by literacy efforts despite some variety of programming and assistance.

The differentiated status of bilingual skills between Anglos and Hispanics, the institutional constraints of public schooling, and the historic underfunding of adult basic education and English literacy illustrate a social institution that operates, intentionally or unintentionally, to deny educational, social, and economic opportunities to an ethnic minority group, thus relegating Hispanics, and in particular Chicanos/as, to the lowest rungs of the economic ladder. Structural discrimination, or institutionalized racism, "assists in the maintaining of minorities in a subordinate position," as Baker (1995) documented in his Idaho study. Inaccessible adult education contributes to Hispanics' difficulty in getting an education, thus restricting full participation in the mainstream society.

Subsequently, Hispanics, as a group, have substantially higher rates of limited English skills in addition to the fewest years of schooling, just over ten years on average, than other racial groups (National Center for Education Statistics 1993), regardless of the measure used. Nationally, large numbers of Mexican Americans leave school without a diploma according to a recent report from the National Council of La Raza (2001). Almost half of Mexican Americans (49 percent) ages twenty-five and over do not have a high school diploma, making it the largest undereducated Hispanic American subgroup. Comparatively, thirty-six percent of Puerto Ricans and 27 percent of Cuban Americans do not have a high school degree.

A recent adult literacy study, the National Adult Literacy Survey (National Center for Education Statistics 1993), indicates that 47 percent of the adult population, or ninety million people, have limited English literacy skills; racially 54 percent of Hispanic Americans, as compared with 44 percent of African Americans, and 15 percent of Anglo Americans. Of those eligible for traditional adult basic education and English literacy services, only 5.9 percent participate (National Center for Education Statistics 1993). Thus, a full 94 percent of eligible adults do not benefit from formal, publically funded programs. "What other area of education could live with such figures?" asks Quigley (1997, 8). The lack of resolve to do away with illiteracy may actually be grounded in stereotyped and discriminatory assumptions that are made about individuals with low literacy skills.

Further Considerations

Families, especially as a social network, have considerable experience with literacy, routinely handling literacy demands in these, as well as other, domains and consistently indicating interest in improving their literacy skills. For example, in one of Chicago's Mexican American communities, English literacy was actively taught by parents within the homes (Farr 1991). English literate adults within the social network were held in high regard. Literacy practices were woven into the fabric of family life. Not only literacy for children, which was linked to schooling opportunities, but literacy for older adults was evidenced by texts in English and Spanish within the community and the home. English literacy training does occur outside mainstream, government-funded programs countering the notion that nonparticipation means literacy education is not taking place. An understanding of cultural values and the context of literacy in the community is required to make sense of this situation.

Participation is a social phenomena embedded in adult development and cultural context. The extent of program participation by individuals is clearly shaped by the realities of adults' lives and responsibilities rather than by student choices (Albert and D'Amico-Samuels 1991). Recorded absences from daily attendance at a multicultural literacy program in the Northeastern United States revolved around work demands, child-rearing, and other life responsibilities. The data from this study help to generate a picture of adult learners as "highly functional" participants in their communities and as embedded in a variety of networks and groups (51). The authors state that research "must be done, however, with full cognizance of the interplay between factors external to adult education programs (such as the changing job market and the availability of day care) and internal aspects of program operation and student participation and achievement...for a more comprehensive understanding of adult learners..." (23).

In one of the few research studies looking specifically at Mexican American enrollments in adult basic education programs in the Southwest, Richardson (1980) found that although Mexican Americans in Texas had more experiences of problematic participation (e.g., more illness, child-care, having to work), their enrollment in programs was greater than their eligible numbers would indicate. Richardson cites a pattern of high Mexican American participation in adult basic education as compared to a significantly lower participation rate by Anglos, three times less than for Mexican Americans. In Colorado, participation in state-administered adult education programs for 1998 indicated that of the total enrolled, 48 percent were Hispanic as opposed to an enrollment rate of 31 percent for Anglos (U.S. Department of Education 1998). With a Hispanic population of 17 percent compared to an Anglo population of 75 percent in Colorado (U.S. Bureau of the Census 2000), it would seem that Hispanic adults are highly motivated to take advantage of educational opportunities and are interested in learning. None of the state reports, such as the one cited for Colorado, however, indicate whether the Hispanic population reported are United States citizens, migrant workers, or immigrants from various Central American and South American countries. With the growing number of Hispanic migrants and immigrants to the United States, the statistics tell little about who is actually enrolled in adult basic education and English literacy programs. In the Southwest, this is a noteworthy consideration because the region is home to a large population of both migrants and Hispanic Americans.

In another national study (Moore and Stavrianos 1995) 45 percent of all new adult basic education clients between the ages of sixteen and fifty-five are nonwhite; Latino origin individuals make up the largest proportion and may reflect the growing English as a Second Language (ESL) population in traditional programs. These studies reflect the commitment by Hispanic, or Latino/a, individuals to engage in adult educational opportunities, but they do not illuminate the underlying factors that influence the resistance of eligible adults who do not enroll in traditional adult programs.

Sociological Perspectives

Placing adult education within the larger structural framework of society and investigating the dynamics between Mexican Americans and the social structures of everyday life is required for an in-depth understanding, including not just schooling, but also other economic, political, social, and cultural settings. The notion of individual choice fails to consider the structural factors that press upon people as they attempt to meet their educational needs. By focusing on the failings of individuals rather than social structures, maintenance of the status quo is ensured. Exploring the issue of adult basic education and English literacy nonparticipation from a critical social perspective, more specifically, from a social action paradigm, affirms the dialectical interplay between social structures and people's experiences of everyday life by constructing a structural-cultural model focusing on the interaction effect between human agency as cultural consciousness and structural determinants of race, ethnicity, and class as historically situated in time and space. Individuals and groups are not simply impacted by social structures, relations, culture and ideology; individuals have the capacity to create their own lives.

This sociological tradition is concerned with the critical analysis of society and societal structures, institutions and mechanisms, yet encompasses divergent theoretical approaches: (1) those that emphasize understanding the reproduction of existing social relationships, and (2) those that emphasize agency and the production of meaning and culture through collective and individual resistance to imposed knowledge and practices. However, what essentially defines critical educational theory is its moral imperative and emphasis on the need for both individual empowerment and social transformation. The paradigm of production and agency where individuals and groups assert their own interests and contest ideological and material forces imposed on them is the perspective employed here.

Production and Agency

Production theories are concerned with the ways individuals and groups assert their own experiences and contest or resist the material and ideological forces imposed upon them in a variety of settings. Critical production theorists in education focus their analysis on how individuals produce meaning and culture through their resistance and their individual and collective consciousness. These theories are concerned with the social construction of knowledge and the various ways knowledge and action can be critiqued and made problematic. There is an equal emphasis on the power of structural determinants such as material practices, modes of power, and economic and political institutions to both enable and constrain social life.

Giddens's (1979, 1984) notions about the dialectic between agency and structure, Structuration Theory, provides a useful paradigm to view complex dynamics of conflict, power, social practices, and structures. Giddens defines structuration as "conditions governing the continuity of transmutation of structures, and therefore the reproduction of social systems" (1984, 25). In other words, a duality of structures exists, an interrelationship between structure and agency (and agency and power). Structures are both medium and outcome, both enabling and constraining, and it is this interconnection between these conditions and the consequences that illuminate the dialectic. Rules and resources are drawn upon by men and women in interaction, but the rules and resources, as well as the identities drawn upon, are reconstituted through such interaction.

Equally important to Giddens is the recursive character of social life mobilized through social practices at levels both discursive, knowledge that is expressed at the level of discourse, and practical, tacit knowledge drawn upon in social activity that cannot be formulated discursively. Discursive consciousness, then, is what can be said; whereas, practical consciousness guides what is simply done.

Relations, practices, ideology, rules, and mechanisms are both generated and reproduced in action. While there is the possibility of social transformation through reflexive monitoring of behavior, the bounds of "knowability" of the agent and the influence of structural constraints directly affect motives and processes of knowing. Social life is formed and reformed in praxis, in the practical activities carried out in the enactment of daily life. Giddens's theory of action, or production, reflects a belief in the agency of individuals as knowing subjects who react to, and act upon, the social world they inhabit. This is not to say that people are always aware of how the social structure impacts them as individuals or as a group, but rather to suggest that most individuals do have a general understanding of their place within the sociocultural environment. For example, those who are tracked into an academic program in high school take for granted they will attend a college that will prepare them for their place in a professional career even if they are not aware how the system works or understand why they would take the situation for granted in the first place. Giddens (1979) maintains that every social actor indeed knows a great deal about the conditions of reproduction of the society in which he or she is a member.

People reflexively monitor not only behaviors but also the setting in which social interaction takes place. Knowing agents, especially "those in subordinate positions in social systems, are frequently adept at converting whatever resources they possess into some degree of control over the conditions of reproduction of those social systems" (6). Individuals engage in strategic conduct. Thus, through monitoring of settings and interactions, contestation and transformation of social structures can occur. In fact, Giddens states, "Those who, in a largely unquestioning way, accept certain dominant perspectives may be more imprisoned within them than others are, even though these perspectives help the former to sustain their position of dominance" (1979, 72).

Giddens's notion of "the acting subject" insists upon an idea of power as two dimensional; it is a resource individuals draw upon as they act on their own behalf. In power struggles, the dialectic of control always operates. Thus, individuals reflexively monitor their conduct via the knowledge they have of the circumstances of their activities. As knowing subjects, individuals engage in strategic conduct based on prior knowledge, experiences, and social constraints. In other words, the notion of action hinges on the acting self located within historically located modes of activity. Further, the very monitoring of activity and behavior indicates intentionality and purpose.

Gramsci's (1971) work has become increasingly influential in critical educational theory because of his analysis of consciousness. Central to his thought is a concern with the various hegemonic ways in which dominant society imposes its concept of reality on all subordinate classes and the possible ways in which the oppressed can create alternative cultural and political institutions to establish their own means to oppose and change society. The ideological development of personality is the result of learning and experiences in all kinds of settings—family, work, church, schools, informal relations. Boggs (1976) interprets Gramsci's view of hegemony as "an organizing principle that is diffused by agencies of ideological control and socialization in everyday life" (39). The sense of hegemony as control for the reproduction of dominant society has led to a reading of Gramsci where every individual is shaped through hegemonic ideas and historical circumstances (Mouffe 1979). Gramsci's (1971) work reveals an insistence on the power of individuals to contest the control of the dominate society and the resulting need for the dominant class to reimpose its worldview since it is in constant danger of being questioned and resisted by subordinate groups.

In addition to his concern with the power of dominant groups to shape the consciousness of subordinate groups, Gramsci insists on the active, critical quality of consciousness and the possibilities inherent in the act of schooling. "The learner is not a passive and mechanical recipient, a gramophone record—even if the liturgical conformity of examinations sometimes makes him appear so. The relation between these educational forms and the child's psychology are always active and creative, just as the relation of the worker to his tools is active and creative" (1971, 42).

Further, Gramsci recognizes individuals as historical products and recognizes the active quality of being. His notion of the "organic intellectual" calls for a philosophy of "critical elaboration" that emerges from an understanding of the common sense world and the historical and economic forces that have shaped it. "The starting-point of critical elaboration is the consciousness of what one really is and in 'knowing thyself' as a product of the historical process to date which has deposited in you an infinity of traces, without leaving an inventory" (326). One author suggests that Gramsci's analysis of the power of hegemonic ideas to shape consciousness, "coupled with his unshakable belief in the power of critique and political activism, allow us to begin to see individuals as both shaped by history and shapers of history" (Weiler 1988, 17).

A Conceptualization of Resistance

Freire (1971, 1985) is committed to a belief in the power of individuals to come to a critical consciousness of their own being in the world. While he sees individuals as determined, he believes they are also able to reflect on that determinism and thus begin to "free themselves." Central to Freire's work is the understanding that individuals are agents, engaged in both the construction and reconstruction of meaning. Thus men and women must seek to understand the forces of hegemony within their own consciousness as well as in the structured, historical circumstances in which they find themselves.

Much of Freire's work has involved literacy education in societies emerging from historical colonialism and imperialism. As the dominant culture strives to encourage negative attitudes toward the culture of the dominated, while at the same time imposing their way of being and doing, tensions mount. In truth, the dominated have been forbidden to be who they are. The ability of an individual to appropriate reality by naming, reading, and therefore knowing that reality, can lead to action and the possibility of transforming reality. This naming of one's reality and the making of meaning can lead to practices of resistance in order to change one's circumstances.

Activities of resistance and reaffirmation strive to invent mechanisms for retaining cultural autonomy while attaining economic and political equality. Freire (1985) refers to these responsive activities as "snaps" or breaking points, "moments of culture." He contends that these "moments of culture" vary in issue and context as violations of knowing. "As more and more things snap, they bring about mobilization. Initially, this mobilization is minimal. But this mobilization keeps increasing as it takes on different issues in different contexts" (192). The dominated take the initiative and develop their own strategies in order to fight oppression. Freire, therefore, gives us a working definition of the concept of resistance: individual and group action, both discursive and nondiscursive, informed by experience and taken to reaffirm and sustain cultural identity.

Educational Inquiry of Structure and Agency

Educational literature investigating social structures and human agency span a period of more than three decades, yet the critical analysis of education as a deeply embedded social institution of society serving both public and private interests remains obscure and inaccessible to the general public.

Giroux's (1983) work applies critical education theory to the question of schooling and attempts to clarify and expand the concepts of ideology, resistance, and hegemony. He addresses schools as both the means of social and cultural reproduction and as sites of the production of individual subjectivities and cultures. Giroux is especially concerned about demonstrating the dialectical nature of social reality.

This concern with structuration reflects a belief in the agency of individuals to react to and act upon the social world they inhabit and insists upon the possibility of social transformation through action. Giroux emphasizes a notion of ideology that exists in "a complex nexus of structural needs, common sense and critical consciousness" (18). Common sense refers to the level of everyday consciousness with its blend of unexamined assumptions, internalized rules and moral codes, and partial insights. The realm of common sense is open to criticism because of the hegemonic ideology it partially embodies; thus, the contradictions of everyday life and consciousness can be examined and transformed.

Different racial, ethnic, class, and gender groups experience the dominate culture and its social structures in materially different ways. The impact of these dynamics placed within and alongside traditional adult basic education programs suggest the struggles Mexican Americans contend with as they attempt to continue their formal learning through adult programs. For example, programs try to "monoculture students" (Vogel Zanger 1994), forbid languages other than English (Sparks 1993), define participant needs rather than acknowledge the experiences of everyday life of adults who can determine their own needs (Horsman 1990), exhibit racial bias (Quigley 1987; Weiss 1983), and assume cultural assimilation for all nondominant groups (Pai 1990; Walsh 1991). Mexican Americans also push against such forces as "space, time, and resources which are usually located outside [their] control and based on the needs of others" (Horsman 1990, 85).

Quigley's (1997) research into resistance helps us understand that African American students quit high school and resist adult education because their ideas of what schooling is about will be repeated in adult education. In an earlier work, Quigley (1987) found that resistance takes place in a predictable series of stages. Using Bourdieu's concepts of habitat, defined as the objectified lessons of schooling; and habitus, defined as values and culture, Quigley found that characters in selected literary works such as *Huckleberry Finn* exhibited intolerance to the schooling habitus of values and culture including the system of dispositions, the manner of being, lifestyles, and normative expectations. None of those characters, however, resisted the schooling habitat of reading, writing, and math lessons. While individuals objected to the transmission of cultural values around schooling, none resisted the actual knowledge base transmitted through schooling. Schooling shapes the individual and has a lifelong affect as McDonald (1974) found in his study. Those who leave school before graduating continue low participation levels in adult education throughout their lives (Cervero and Fitzpatrick 1990). Based on disparate realities between Mexican Americans and other nondominant groups, the school's culture and structure creates an inability to accommodate the basic realities of the lives of students (Baker 1996). Stuckey (1991) goes further by exposing the violence of literacy by stating that "literacy is a social restriction and an individual accomplishment" (64). We must focus on the conditions of the literacy process that determine possible outcomes of academic success and cultural sensitivity.

Perhaps one of the best known studies of cultural production was conducted by Willis (1977) in the study of counterschool cultures with working-class boys in London. His concern was with how working-class identity is reproduced in the individual and in the group and actively lived as an everyday experience, thus recreating and applying this situated identity to new situations. Using the concept of resistance to explore the interaction of agency and structure, Willis uncovered some of the mechanisms by which class culture is reproduced, as well as ways in which the working-class lads resisted hegemonic ideology and power while ironically helping to reproduce it. Through their attitudes of disdain for school and the intellectuals, their skipping of classes and hanging out, they created a subculture of resistance. Willis argues that the starting point for an investigation of the interface of the individual and the social should be the cultural sphere, "in material practices and productions, in lives in their historical context in the everyday span of existence and practical consciousness" (49). He sees that the cultural production of identity is not specifically individual, but collective, as is the expression of class experience and its relationship to economic and political institutions.

A study of young Puerto Rican children found that the effects of island colonialism resonates within the collective memories of reconstructed social, economic, cultural, racial, linguistic, and political conflicts; these historical conflicts are internalized in language and in consciousness (Walsh 1991). These Puerto Rican children learned English, yet demonstrated understandings of English texts and tests that were divergent from native English speakers. In the United States, the English language is often characterized as the unifying thread of generations of immigrants with an implied system of shared cultural values. While English may bring people together, it does not unify the diverse and multiple experiences and realities of racial, ethnic, class, and gender groups. How the past and present intersect in people's voices frames the conditions and processes involved in coming to know. Colonialism, as a structural relationship between dominant and oppressed groups, impacts upon individual and group identity formation through material and ideological constraints operating in complex and reinforcing ways.

Weiss (1983), in her comparative work with African American and white community college students, investigated schooling and cultural production. The students were from lower-class backgrounds coming from families that were economically marginalized and permanently trapped. Weiss indicates the students were aware of this and actively perceived "Urban College as a mediator between two worlds—the 'streets' and the cultural mainstream" (237). Students viewed the institution as a way of escaping aspects of their immediate environment. Weiss's study participants "criticized their teachers insofar as they did not encourage what the students considered a fair transaction. In return for respect or obedience on the part of students, faculty were expected to share their knowledge" (241). In other words, urban college students approved of what the teachers had to offer, they simply wanted them to offer it, and they held teachers responsible for student failure. Further, these students not only see knowledge as power but "college knowledge has an immediacy and potency that is readily verbalized" (244); it leads directly to personal enhancement and collective improvement. Perceiving that teachers are not dedicated, there is limited communication between students and teachers. As a result of perceived notions of cultural and racial bias exhibited by teachers and that knowledge is not evenly distributed, the students respond through high absenteeism, high withdrawals and associated drop out. This behavior directly contradicts their attitudes toward knowledge and schooling. This pattern of dropping in and out must be seen as a response toward their position within society and the living conditions of its members. This behavior indicates a creative response to a set of conditions both inside and outside the institution. Weiss argues that the logic examined in her study is a group logic necessarily seen in a specific historical relation. Although not predetermined nor conscious, it is, also, not accidental.

In a study of English literacy and lower-class women in Nova Scotia, Horsman (1990) found that the material conditions and the complexity of the women's everyday experiences were effectively obscured as standard English was presented as simply correct English rather than a class-based language, where needs of participants were defined by experts, and where teaching was conducted as an individualized activity rather than creating the social interaction most of these women wanted. "Literacy and training programs are part of a process which classifies people as deficient, individualizes their problems, and offers a remedy that ensures the status quo is maintained" (217). The Nova Scotia women appeared to resist the power of the discourses (motivation, choice, functionality, needs) that defined them as outsiders, incompetent, and stupid, by either negotiating what they needed from the programs or by dropping out. These women reflect the inconsistencies and contradictions of class-based and gender-based experiences that exist alongside the Eurocentric ethos. Likewise, these women illustrate how individuals in a social position other than the mainstream are created as objects of discrimination, shaped by those threatened with difference, and appropriated as strange, exotic, and inferior.

Fine's (1989) work in New York high schools illuminates the standard educational practices of silencing student and community voices as individuals attempt to articulate their lives. As she began her study with high school dropouts, the principal of the school warned her not to use the words "dropping out" to students because, "If you say it, you encourage them to do it" (156). Not naming is an administrative craft that serves to preserve the ideology of equal opportunity and access while masking the unequal distribution of resources; creates the impression of democracy and collaboration within a system of unequal power relations; quiets student voices of difference and dissent while appropriating them as deviant and dangerous; and removes from public discourse the tensions that exist as evidenced by failure as a majority experience for low income individuals. Also removed from public discourse are the private interests that are mediated through the public sphere of schooling and the broken promises of social and economic mobility.

Fine identifies the process of splitting the personal and the social voice whereby she means social problems are managed as personal problems inside school offices of counselors or psychologists. "The offices of school psychologists and counselors therefore become the primary sites for addressing what were indeed social concerns, should have been academic concerns, and were most likely to be managed as personal and private concerns. The privatizing and psychologizing of public and political issues served to reinforce the alienation of students' lives from their educational experiences" (165).

As thoroughly silenced as students may be, they retained the energy, persistence, and even resistance that fuel a willingness to keep trying to get a hearing. Students probed teachers they didn't agree with, challenged the experiences of these authorities, and actively spoofed the class and race biases that routinely structured classroom activities. Efforts by teachers "to shut down conversations were usually followed by the counting of money by males, the application of mascara or lipstick by females, and the laying down of heads on desks by students of both genders: the loss of control over the classroom" (159). Instead of seeing dropping out as individual acts, expressions of incompetence, or self sabotage, Fine views dropping out as initially filled with energy, vision, and resisting agency. Efforts of the larger society to mute individual voices about public social problems are simultaneously successful, nevertheless.

Another study looked at bilingual Hispanic students enrolled in a college skills class who were asked to help non-Hispanic teachers in their school gain a better understanding of their needs (Vogel Zanger

1994). As academically successful students who shared a commitment to finishing high school and going on to college, these individuals, nonetheless, had to contend with numerous and ongoing obstacles to the attainment of that success. Struggling against teacher bias and racism, exclusion of Hispanic cultures and history from the curriculum, as well as teacher mistrust and lack of teacher support, these students resisted cultural assimilation and submissive attitudes as a precondition for literacy development. Vogel Zanger contends "literacy development may be constrained by the schools' failure to take advantage of the cultural capital that linguistic minority students bring to school" (185). The continued presence of the students in school despite debilitating social experiences, attests to their active engagement in reaching their educational goals of going to college.

Failure to incorporate a student's language and culture results in responses of student withdrawal and resistance to stigmatized ethnic or social class identity as well. "The school is communicating to this group of students a strongly subtractive context, which they resent. One student coins a new phrase in condemning the school's attempt to monoculture her and her Hispanic peers. Students sense that their culture is under attack, that it will be lost if they do not defend it" (181). Vogel Zanger warns that more linguistic-minority students may be driven to drop out if schools continue to ignore the perspectives of nondominant culture students.

Fowler-Frey (1996) reminds us that literacy learners have assumptions about teaching and learning just as teachers have expectations. The difference, however, is that learners' assumptions are based on past educational experiences or as a result of no past educational experiences. Based on the high cultural value put on print literacy in the United States, both native and nonnative linguistic minority adults have often been excluded from participating in society because they do not have the literacy skills society expects them to have.

In summary, responses to material and ideological forces imposed upon individuals document the multiple ways people assert their experiences and contest, or resist, dominant culture. Groups represented in these studies include members from various racial, class, and gender positions. Forms of cultural production, both discursive and nondiscursive, include the following: creation of subcultures; silence; verbal challenges and questions; alternative English language styles and discourse forms; indirect withdrawal from learning; absenteeism; criticism of teachers as authority; negotiation of perceived educational needs; withdrawal from educational programs; valuation of different class, ethnic, and gender cultures; and academic success. This literature suggests factors that may contribute to the struggle that many groups have, including Mexican American adults, especially when seeking to get an education. What kinds of conditions have they encountered? Have their educational experiences been similar to individuals in these studies? These questions are cause for concern not only because of the dramatic increase in the numbers of Mexican Americans in the United States as shown in the latest census, but because of the very question of social relations, power, and forms of oppression.

Research Questions and Qualitative Fieldwork

I initiated the study by looking for Mexican American adults not enrolled in adult basic education and English literacy programs because all of the nonparticipation studies that try to explain why people do not participate have been conducted with the relatively small number of people already enrolled in programs.

To continue to rely on studies that survey participating adults to understand issues of nonparticipation is to make invisible the disproportionately large number of adults who are eligible for services but who are not served. Likewise, these studies, by ignoring the problems faced by nonparticipants in adult basic education and English literacy programs, mask the fact that the United States has one of the lowest literacy rates among industrialized nations and ranks forty-ninth in literacy among 158 members of the United Nations (Carmack 1992). There is the necessity of "understanding nonparticipation from the perspective of the nonparticipant as well as the broader social dynamics that so influence the formation of that perspective" (Rockhill 1983, 27).

This study investigated the historical contexts of education, learning, and literacy (Spanish and English) experiences of Mexican American adults. There were three characterizing dimensions of the study. A microethnographic strategy (Berg 1989) was used to explain how historical and contemporary events, perceptions, and meanings interplay to result in the struggle for an adequate education. Microethnography focuses on particular "incisions," or slices of life, at particular points in the larger setting and, in turn, points to important aspects of life in the larger group or collective. The second influence is a feminist methodology that centers individuals as subjects of knowledge rather than as objects of knowledge. It is grounded in understanding historical subjectivity, a knowledge that "begins with an awareness of our relationship to the historical contexts in which we live" (Westcott 1983, 395).

The third is a cross-cultural approach that emphasizes the need for sensitivity to, and value for, difference, as well as the significance of the subjective culture of the group. A cross-cultural methodology views research as a shared human experience with the potential for understanding cultural difference and the normality of pluralism (Stanfield 1993, Marin and Marin 1989). As an Anglo, middle-class female, this project required me to pay particular attention to ascriptive categories of race, class, and gender. As a result, I sought sponsorship from Mexican Americans in several community agencies who introduced me to potential participants. I recruited a translator in each community and developed a two-tiered translation scheme. Further, I had the collected data reviewed by several key Chicano/a informants to clarify accuracy, ethnic meaning, and subsequent findings.

Individuals described their efforts to reach their educational goals as youth and adults. Information was derived from having participants discuss three general areas: their past childhood schooling, their efforts to reach their educational goals, and the decisions and actions they have taken regarding adult basic education and English literacy programs.

Data were collected over a ten-month period using participant observation (Jorgensen 1989, Lincoln and Guba 1985) and in-depth interviewing. The data collection began as soon as I entered the field in November, 1993, and concluded at the beginning of August, 1994, with more than 140 hours of observation conducted in community centers, employment service agencies, adult education centers, and public community locations. Observation entails the systematic description of events, actions, and objects found in the social location of the study (Lofland and Lofland 1984). This method was used as the beginning point to assist in getting a lay of the land. Specifically, moving around in the community and in the Chicano/a neighborhoods, plus witnessing public events, oriented me to the study and informed the structuring of the interview process. I focused on economic, social, and political conditions, and the interactions of individuals and groups as they reflected literacy skills and language. Data were collected regarding the differential economic conditions of neighborhood alleys, streets, and yards; housing units; types of services and businesses, including a number of locally owned and operated Spanish language businesses; election placards and billboards. Collection of Hispanic community newspapers (i.e., La Voz, Hispania News), handbills from community organizations, and other documents; attendance at social and public events (i.e., Unity Day, Cinco de Mayo) held in the Mexican American communities; and visitation to public spaces including Mexican American community parks, theaters, and museums facilitated a multidimensional picture of the communities. Informal interviews were conducted with Mexican American leaders in the Colorado Springs and Denver communities to gain their perspectives of the everyday situations there. Community providers and leaders included adult educators, directors of community centers, a drug counselor, parent advocates from two different school districts, members of local chapters of the GI Forum and the Chicano Unity Council, and a Catholic priest. I also served meals at community centers, tutored Hispanic students in adult education programs, and assisted clients in filling out application forms at employment service agencies; observed family interaction during interview sessions; and spent social, informal time with some of the study participants at public community events in both Colorado Springs and Denver.

A simple criterion-based selection was used to identify participants for the study. Individuals were Mexican American adults, 18 years or older, born in the United States, without a high school diploma, and not enrolled in adult basic education, English literacy, or GED preparation. Thirty individuals were recruited through local agencies and personal introductions. They were interviewed in two large urban communities in Colorado, Colorado Springs and Denver; twenty-two were women and eight were men. Most were third generation Americans; some were fourth-generation. All were of mixed Spanish, Indian, and Mexican heritage. The majority were bilingual Spanish and English, all preferred to use English for the interviews even though a translator was available.

A four-part interview guide with questions about educational history, ethnic identity, Spanish language experiences and background, and the decisions and actions taken regarding participation in adult basic education and English literacy was developed (Seidman 1991). Interviews were conducted in community centers, family-owned businesses, homes, and governmental agencies. All interviews were audio-tape recorded and transcribed verbatim.

The data analysis itself proceeded according to the constant comparative method whereby collection, coding, and analysis occur jointly in order to develop theory as it emerges (Glaser and Strauss 1967). Grounded theory emerged in the form of key findings. Operational categories were replaced or enhanced with emergent constructs. Initial coding revealed analytical categories pertaining to individuals' educational efforts. Each cogent response involved the individual's assessment of the learning environment or the teaching-learning exchange. Comparisons among the individual cases began to set the data in the larger social context. Finally, key linkages among bounded categories were identified. Findings depicted experiences of conflict, not only in schools but in other social settings, limited access to resources, isolation from the mainstream culture, and differential treatment in work, social, and other environments.

Some may challenge that a white woman has no business conducting a study with Mexican Americans since I can never hope to fully understand their perspectives. I initiated this study out of concern that as a veteran practitioner of adult basic education programs in predominately Mexican American communities I needed to know as much as possible about those with whom I worked if I were to truly help them reach their goals. My background and positionality influence how I experience and perceive the world, just as the historical colonization and the subsequent lived experiences influence those who participated in this project. Through my efforts, I attempt to understand as best I can how people make sense of their world. The importance of doing cross cultural work, in my view, outweighs the limitations of my positionality. Understanding and valuing those who are different from me requires my engagement in the struggle to find spaces where we can come together for dialogue. I think it is important for people to speak for themselves, subsequently, I have used their words to describe their lived experiences and perceptions of those experiences. My intention here is to provide a space, an opening, for them to speak, and I have included my interpretation separately. This is a rendering of what I saw and heard and how I make sense of it all.

Schooling, and by extension adult education, is not an isolated site of everyday life but is embedded in larger social structures of meaning. How adult education functions to differentiate, separate, and impede full social, mainstream participation for Mexican Americans can be seen in specific sociocultural practices as experienced by the men and women who participated in this study. As they have struggled throughout their lives to get an education, we catch glimpses into the strength of agency as people press against the social structures, practices, and mechanisms of education, the economy, and the political and cultural imperatives of the dominant culture.

As I mentioned earlier, while structures press upon and maintain social life, individuals reflexively monitor their conduct via the knowledge they have of the circumstances of their activities (Giddens 1979). As knowing subjects, individuals engage in strategic action, or "moments of culture," based on prior knowledge, experiences, and social constraints. The very monitoring of activity and behavior indicates intentionality and purpose, however, this is not to say that these individuals are always successful. Group logic sustains an oppositional cultural frame of reference that is learned more or less unconsciously by caste-like minorities (those incorporated into a society more or less involuntarily and permanently through conquest, slavery, or colonization) (Ogbu 1987). How individual Chicanos/as perceive opportunities based on cultural background and political situation has more to do with academic success than language, difference, cognitive style, or culture. Cultural inversion, whereby some members of nondominant groups claim other forms of behaviors, events, symbols, and meanings as appropriate for them because these are not characteristic of another group, is sometimes used to challenge negative stereotypes or derogatory images attributed by the dominant group.

Gramsci's (1971) concept of hegemony, or predominant authority, helps us analyze the various ways in which dominant society imposes its concept of reality on all subordinate groups and the possible ways in which the oppressed can establish their own means to oppose and change it. The ideological consciousness is formed not through informal institutions, but rather through the formal apparatus, the schools. The education system appears as a privileged instrument for the socialization of a hegemonic culture. The formation and regulation of dominant social, economic, cultural, and political ideas in individual consciousness is a continuous process of reaffirmation, yet is always capable of being resisted.

The interaction effect of structures and agency on one side and culture and identity formation on the other side, therefore, provides a critical forum in which to investigate the embedded issues of nonparticipation and people's efforts to meet their educational needs and desires.

Chapter 2

Faces of Struggle

> I am Joaquin, lost in a world of confusion, caught up in the
> whirl of a gringo society, confused by the rules, scored by atti-
> tudes, suppressed by manipulation, and destroyed by modern
> society. (Gonzales 1972, 6-7)

I began my investigation by tutoring Hispanic adults in reading at an adult basic education program sponsored by the local school district in a small interracially mixed neighborhood of Colorado Springs. The instructors were happy to have me there since adults who are learning to read and write are at various levels of proficiency making it more difficult to have large classrooms of people working together. I would work with small groups of three and four Hispanic students, some from Mexico, some from El Salvador or Guatemala. There were often Mexican Americans in the groups as well. From them I learned about the neighborhood, the places they shopped, the streets they lived on, the atmosphere of the city. They talked about conditions in their children's schools and the jobs they held during the day. Having taught in similar programs for many years, I used the adult basic education program as an anchor to my being in the community. When I wasn't teaching, I visited community centers or met with Mexican American leaders from churches and other social organizations looking for people to potentially participate in the study. While teaching I often asked students if they knew Mexican Americans who had not finished school and who might talk to me.

Finding Chicanos/as who had not finished school was more difficult than simply going to the adult basic education program and asking people to participate in a study. We have no way of determining if the person standing next to us in the grocery line has not completed school and is eligible for adult basic education services, nor did I initially know, as an outsider, where I might find people willing to talk to me.

Mexican Americans who are eligible for adult basic education services live a variety of lifestyles. I met people who were successful small business owners who were introduced to me by community agency directors. I met women on public assistance who were picking up food stamps at the outreach office. I met elderly men and women who ate their meals at the local community center a couple days a week. I met construction workers who were searching for work at the job service center, and I met the relatives and friends of students I worked with at the adult basic education program. All of these people were eligible to attend adult basic education or English literacy programs because of self-identified low-level skills in reading, writing, or mathematics. Remembering that 94 percent of adults eligible for adult basic education and English literacy services do not participate, it should not be surprising that this population of people can be found everywhere yet nowhere in particular.

Fifty-five people were asked to participate in the study and discuss with me their experiences, decisions, and subsequent actions regarding education; in the end, thirty agreed. They were a diverse group of individuals in age, family migration history, political views, educational attainment and experiences, gender, religious background, family composition, goals and aspirations. As I previously mentioned, there were twenty-two women and eight men between the ages of eighteen to sixty-two. Six people were from Colorado Springs; the remainder, twenty-four, were from Denver. The majority were bilingual Spanish and English; there were no monolingual Spanish speakers, and some individuals would describe their Spanish language abilities as "enough to get around." Their commonalities included their ethnicity; all were Mestizos, of mixed Spanish, Indian, and Mexican blood; they all were born in the United States; they all talked of racial discrimination, yet the venues varied; and they all told stories of unsatisfying educational histories. In order to get a better feel for the people who participated in the study, profiles of five individuals are presented; profiles that highlight personal perceptions and experiences while showing variations across generations and genders.

I have chosen to use verbatim quotations from individuals who shared their stories with me. Rather than sanitize their language by converting it to standardized and privileged usage, I believe it is important to hear people in their own words. In my view this does not diminish, in any way, the individual, their ability to articulate their lives, or the reader's ability to understand what people are saying.

Olivia: It's a Matter of Difference

> I went to an all Mexican school; it was in the Hispanic part of town, that's where all your Chicanos lived, the majority of students were Chicanos. My son didn't [go to an all Mexican school] and had a total different outlook, and I'll tell you I noticed the difference. [The Anglo students] had more opportunity, 'cause see, I got to make it one year. My parents moved at the time and I started going [to the white school] even though I wasn't quite set up for it.

Olivia grew up in the beet fields working with her family. The Mexican schools she was familiar with were segregated schools designated especially for the children of the farm workers. When she was high school age, her family moved from the colonia, a residential area created for farm workers, to the city where new opportunities opened up for her including access to white schools. So at a late point in Olivia's educational years, she had the chance to compare the two distinct types of segregated schools. Having such an opportunity, she came to know, first-hand, the different life she and her family members had lived in the colonia versus the city. Because of this experience, she also knew the opportunities her children would have living in the city, and she felt that her son had a very different perspective of schooling than she did.

I had already come from this rough background of Chicanos that belonged to little [gangs]. That's how I knew the difference. You get into a school like that and it's just so different, the teaching is different. You can't quite put your thumb on it, the politeness. There was more offered compared to my high school, a big difference.

Not once did anybody ever talk to me about catching up or that we'd begin with a tutor; it was never a big thing to press on about education. For some reason, it was with the whites, the ones that got behind. I remember one girl, she went back to school, the teachers went down and talked with her parents. Well, they probably just didn't see that there was any hope for us.

Olivia points out the differences between what she called the "Mexican school" that she attended for part of her secondary school years and a "white" school she went to for a short time before leaving school. She confirms her knowledge by referring to her son's high school experiences at an integrated school. She noticed that teacher attitudes and priorities differed between the two types of schools and went on to tell of different classes and social activities she had the opportunity to take at the "white" school that were not available to her before, such as outdoor science labs. She believed her son's advantage in attending a racially mixed school gave him an outlook on life that was different from her own.

Olivia is a forty-six-year-old third generation Mestizo who worked in the fields as a young girl. She and her family worked the sugar beet fields for a Jewish family in Greeley, Colorado, and for the Great Western Sugar Company. Olivia's father was the foreman. They lived in a colonia, which was separated from the center of town. Raised in a family of nine children, she was the middle child, the fourth child of her father who left the family within days of her birth. Her mother remarried and another five children were born and raised along with Olivia and her older siblings.

The household was bilingual, although Olivia lost most of her Spanish and did not teach it to her children. She commented that her parents speak more English now than Spanish and that her own children don't know much Spanish. "I wish I would have kept up with my Spanish a lot more. I understand every word but my kids didn't learn it. I didn't teach them because they say you don't live in Mexico so why do you need to know the other language? We're living in the United States, English is the only language that you really need to know so why bother to teach Spanish to your kids?" While some believe that language is one's identity, Olivia believes that culture is identity. "We still have the culture, everything about it. We just don't always use the Spanish speaking. I think it's just a gift, it's just something beautiful that you could know the two languages. I don't think it's so much in the language. My mom tried to implant that [our culture] is us."

Olivia married at seventeen and had two children. She divorced and remarried, having a third child with her second husband. She followed the traditional gender roles, expecting her husband to work and provide for their financial needs while she stayed home with the children. Olivia commented that she trained her children the same way; her two daughters do not work outside the home. Yet, periodically through adulthood, Olivia tried her hand at various jobs to bring in extra money. Working at a child care center, she decided to take courses so she could become certified as a home-based child care center, but she never completed the sequence of required courses. At another point, she cleaned office buildings with a friend to earn extra money to buy furnishings for her home. She also thought of going into counseling so she enrolled in a course at a Hispanic women's center, but she was so turned off by the teacher that she dropped that idea. Frustrated, Olivia went from one thing to another always feeling that she was too stupid, "the dumb little Spanish girl, nothing could be done for me but I feel cheated that I don't have that piece of paper" signifying high school completion. When she was about seventeen, one of her brothers wanted to send her to beauty school. "He figured I had the knack already, I'm going to send her to it. But there again, because of my low self-esteem, of thinking that I could never do anything;" she declined the offer. As Olivia tried her hand at the various vocational courses, spurred on by immediate interests, she found herself in situations with Anglo teachers who could not relate to Hispanics or who were unskilled in teaching to different learning styles.

> I still like to work on hair; I still like to counsel with people. That's why I wanted to see if I could get a job. I would like to learn how to be a receptionist or where you look up files and answer the phone and all that. But see there again, because I'm not well-educated, I've never been a great speller. Anyway, how am I going to go back? I'd have to go so far back, I

don't want to anymore. See I can't just jump in where I want now. Why can't I just take a few classes in what I'm good at and why do I have to backtrack all the way to where they want me to get a GED?

Olivia lives with her family in a working-class Chicano neighborhood in Denver where they own a modest brick home with a yard filled with flowering bushes, plants, and trees, which she proudly pointed out as she walked me to my car at the end of our second interview. Her husband works as a landscaper for the parks and recreation department for the city of Aurora, a suburb of Denver, and created the beauty of the yard. Olivia told me a story about her husband's job to illustrate her understanding of further differentials between her life and neighborhood and the suburban middle-class neighborhoods where her husband often works. "When we went up to the reservoir, my husband was taking me to all the places where he had worked for the city. He gets all over. He goes, 'I want you to see this park,' and when I looked over there I was surprised, it was so beautiful. He goes, 'It's not what you know it's who you know. These people out here are rich people; they know the right people. They know the mayor, they know where to go to get them to okay these things to have their beautiful parks and all that.' I mean I just could not believe it. And he goes, 'Hey, money still talks, and so do white people.'"

The contradictions and the conflicts of Olivia's life revolve around wanting something she feels she has been denied yet backing away from opportunities that might help her reach some of her desires. Raised to believe she was special by her mother, who was able to shield her children from the poverty and intensity of the beet fields, her everyday life experiences would tell her otherwise, based on differential treatment as a member of a minority group. She vacillates between indulging in her low self-esteem and relying on her knowledge of the structural differences that she witnesses in her own life and the lives of her family thus keeping herself stuck in between. According to Olivia, "[Chicanos are] starting to realize we don't need to be like this. We can be just as well-trained and educated as the next guy. And I've noticed in the last fifteen to twenty years Chicanos have come a long ways, let me tell you. Big time, it's a big difference. For me, from the way I was raised, I would like to see more opportunity."

Olivia's ability to reflect on and critique her own educational opportunities as well as her children's, her immediate surroundings and
community, and her lifestyle and culture provide her with the ability to
see change or, perhaps, even transformation in the social position of
Chicanos/as. Nevertheless, she is acutely aware of what remains to be
done to improve the status of her group. Growing up in the poverty of a
migrant colonia has left deeply embedded traces of justified anger and
hopeful desire for a better future.

Carlos: A Survivor Searching for His Place

> I just don't want my kids to drop out like me. I want them to
> get an education and be whatever they want to be. I'm not
> going to force them to do anything, but I never graduated,
> and I always had bad grades. I lost out. I want to get better
> work, into a career, go into a field, that's what I'm trying to
> do. A lot of places you can't get a job, you know, if you don't
> have a diploma or anything, it's hard, so you have to first
> build your reputation. I work at a parts counter for a distrib-
> uting factory for kitchen countertops. Before I got this job, I
> was making countertops, over off 15th and Broadway, that's
> how I got this job.

Carlos is a twenty-one-year-old father of three children, two of
whom are infant twins. I met him, along with his friend Anita, at her
family's grocery store, a lively place of conversation with the feeling of
the local gathering spot. The meeting was arranged for me by a Chicana
agency coordinator I came to know who was concerned about these
two young people who had left school. Anita was asked by her father to
help someone in the grocery store so Carlos and I walked over to the ad-
joining restaurant in order to have a place to sit and talk. It had been an
intensely hot day, all the windows and doors were flung wide open with
the early evening light filtering through; ranchero music played softly
on the jukebox, and there was a solitary middle-aged Latino sitting at
the bar.

Carlos talked of the grief that he caused his parents as he was growing up. "I used to give my mom a lot of grief always running around. She
was always stressed out 'cause I was always doing something," including
getting in trouble with the law. He attempted to finish high school several times but told me, "I dropped out in '91, the year I was supposed to

graduate. I was a junior, I was a junior for three years. I like going to school, it's just the way I got treated a lot of the times." Carlos had tried schools in three different communities, including an alternative high school, and even went all the way to a rich mountain community to attend night school and work construction during the day, but twice he was labeled "a trouble maker" and was kicked out.

The mountain community employed a lot of Mexicans and Mexican Americans to fill its service sector and booming economy but had no available low-rent housing and was not eager to have the workers live in the immediate community. Carlos had to live many miles away, but at least he had a roof over his head, unlike those who filled the campgrounds or slept by the side of the road. He experienced a lot of prejudice, and the unwelcoming attitude of the people finally forced him back to his hometown neighborhood. Knowing that he could attend public school until the age of twenty-one, he tried to get back into his home high school, but the principal would not let him return. At that point, he gave up. Carlos told me, "I wanted to go to the Marines, that was my goal, but I never graduated. You know, I'm an upright guy, and I'm trying to keep my life together here."

As we talked further about work and education, Carlos admitted that on job applications he would sometimes put down that he had a diploma to increase his chances. "Better my chances; but I guess that really don't have nothing to do with it. I guess it has to do with your attitude and your personality." He was equally aware that there are racial preferences in hiring. He told me:

> There's a lot of people that will hire a lot of white people before Mexicans, and sometimes they'll put the Mexicans down and just put up the white people. I like to take the challenge, I mean if that was the only thing I had to go for was working with nothing but Mexicans, I'd do it. I mean, there ain't nothing wrong with it, I've been working with different colored and foreign people.

Carlos lives in Denver's old Mexican American neighborhood, Globeville, preferring it to the other neighborhoods he tried living in to finish high school. Since the age of seventeen, he has worked in construction or construction-related jobs similar to his father and grandfather who both worked construction in Colorado. He was raised in a bilingual household, but Spanish was his first language.

When I was in elementary, I was in bilingual classes. My parents liked it that I was bilingual, but they wanted me to learn Spanish; that was my first language.

Now in the workplace, Carlos is the only one who speaks Spanish and can help out the Spanish-speaking customers. "I get a lot of customers that come in who speak Spanish and I help them because people who work there don't know no Spanish. I'm the only person there that speaks Spanish. I help out whenever I'm here [at the restaurant] too, just help out."

When I asked him what his culture means to him, Carlos indicated that he has pride in his culture but felt he could not explain it. "I don't really know what culture means, but the bilingual has a lot to do with it 'cause you can get by with the Spanish and English; I mean it's good to learn." He remembers his parents telling him to respect his elders and respect himself. "If you don't respect yourself, you ain't going to respect others." He told me, "Chicano is what I was brought up as; that's who I am, what I did in the past, what I do."

Carlos is a young man with many years ahead of him so we could say that the struggle he is having, finding his place in society, is a natural process of young adulthood. The place that has been reserved for him, that of an outsider to the mainstream, however, is not where he wants to be. Yet he seems to retain the right to do it his way, immersing himself in his culture and living according to the values he grew up with, values of responsibility and caring, respect for difference and pride in who he is.

Maria: Living in Two Cultures

When we moved to Colorado [from New Mexico], I didn't know how to talk English. I learned by listening to other people, and I was just interested to learn, just a little bit here and there, you know, just from asking, making mistakes, but I learned. My brothers were talking English, and I picked up there and listening to the radio.

I was introduced to Maria by her daughter-in-law, a student at the adult basic education center where I volunteered as a tutor. Maria agreed to meet with me and her daughter-in-law at the local community center where she went to meet her friends. The two spoke to one another in Spanish. I let Maria know that I was comfortable with her speaking Spanish, although I could not speak fluently and would rely on her daughter-in-law to translate for me. Maria told me she spoke English to people who spoke English including some of her friends, but it was clear she was not as comfortable speaking English as she was speaking Spanish. Nevertheless, she would only use her English with me, an outsider and stranger in her life. At different points in the interview sessions, I wondered if she needed to speak English in order to show me she could.

We met privately in her home for the second interview. I arrived just as her husband was leaving for work. We talked outside for a bit, and Maria told me about her neighbors. Most of them had lived there for a long time; everyone knew one another and helped out when things needed to be done, especially yard work for the elderly. While Maria and her husband owned their home, some of the homes were rented and she pointed to one across the street where two young men had recently moved in. She suspected them of being involved in some kind of trouble because the police had been there the week before, and she was subsequently worried that now there were people living around her whom she did not know. She took me through the house and down to the basement where she had her sewing, and a small inventory of health products which she sold. It was a cozy space with a small kitchen table and chairs in one corner where we sat, an easy chair and couch covered with colorful afghan quilts, and baskets of fabric next to an older model sewing machine. This was obviously her space, where she conducted her business. As we began, Maria told me, "It's weird because all my life it's been in my mind; I always wanted to make a story of my life, way back then, and now it scares me. It scares me sometime just to think [about it]. My boys don't know a lot of the things that I've been through."

Indeed, Maria has lived a hard life shrouded in fear of being taken advantage of, first at the hands of her mother who left all family responsibility to her, then by a jealous husband who watched whatever she did. "He turned to be very jealous. People didn't know me, and they didn't know him. They used to say what a beautiful daughter and he would get mad and more jealous and more jealous. And when we used to g[et] home he'd let me have it." After twenty-some years of marriage, she left the man who abused her, and two years later married again to another man who denied her money and questioned her spending habits. Gender roles learned at an early age in a culture that values the dual responsibilities of production in the home and in the fields surfaced over and over for Maria, yet she lived within these cultural conditions by creating a life of survival of her own design by working outside the house, learning another language, and encouraging her own children to stay in school in order to get better jobs. All but one of her seven children finished high school, and "they know they can go to college if they want."

Maria migrated with her family of eleven siblings from Santa Rosa, New Mexico, to Holly, Colorado, after her grandfather lost a small piece of land they worked, and her father had trouble finding and keeping work to sustain the family. Her father laid railroad tracks in eastern New Mexico for a while, but lost his job to cheaper Chinese labor. It was at that time that he moved his family up to Colorado to do farm work. "When we was in Santa Rosa, my dad didn't have no job, and one morning he listened to the radio and all the farms in Colorado were putting ads on the radio; they needed people to come and work in the fields, beets, sugar beets. So, my dad, one morning was having breakfast and listening to the radio, and he told my mom, 'Well you know what, they're going to pay us to come over and do farm work.' My daddy had to go and we just moved the family over here. They had a house for us, and that's the way we got to the farm."

Maria, the oldest, was responsible for raising the other children and taking care of her father. She made sure her brothers and sisters went to school, but Maria had no formal schooling experiences beyond a few days here and there because her labor was needed to help the family. She was kept busy working in the beet fields during the day and in the house at night. Everything she learned, she "learned outside of school."

> I was the oldest in the family, and my mom never sent me to school. I went to school for maybe one day out of the week when I was about six, seven, then I didn't go at all. I don't know a lot about school because I never went. I had to do the cooking and the cleaning and everything so I stayed home. I used to send all my brothers and sisters to school. I was sure they got on the bus and they had their lunch. I stayed home and worked in the fields, worked in the home. Most of the time I was embarrassed, I didn't have any friends. I just feel

like I didn't want to be in school. I'd rather stay home because I didn't learn nothing. I didn't do what the other kids
were doing. If I would have went every day, I would have
love[ed] it because I think I would have learned.

Santa Rosa, at that time, was a Spanish-speaking community, and
the only Anglos were a few shop owners who also spoke the local Spanish. English was not part of Maria's world in New Mexico. "When we
moved to Colorado, I didn't know how to talk English, here's where I
learned." She would listen to the English-speaking people in the local
grocery store and try to speak it after being reprimanded for speaking
Spanish. At thirteen she ran away from the drudgery of raising her
mother's children and married the foreman of the farm. Although her
father protested, the owner of the farm got a lawyer on behalf of the
foreman who met with her father. There was no protesting after that.
Maria moved into "the big house" with her Mexican husband who read
her comic books, gave her a radio to listen to, and taught her to speak
English. "I learned by seeing and asking questions and everything." She
had women to talk to and formed friendships through house parties.
"There used to be house parties, and I made them understand and I did
too; and I learned to talk English." She no longer had to work in the
fields, although she cleaned houses for Anglo families who also assisted
her with her oral literacy skills. Reflecting back on those times Maria
told me, "My husband should have put me in school, I was only
thirteen."

At fifty-seven Maria cannot read English and continues to look for
people who can help her with her literacy skills. "Help me, help me. I
can't ask for help. I try, but I can't. I don't know how to read and write. I
can't make it," she pleaded as she recounted her trials with learning to
read and write. She had a tutor from her church for a while, but the
woman stopped coming to the house where they had their tutoring sessions. Her daughter, one of seven surviving children, "does the writing.
She takes me a lot of places. She helps me read my letters and write out
my checks." In public places, such as the grocery store, she gets clerks to
read for her or write her checks by feigning, "I'm sorry I forgot my
glasses." Maria is an intelligent woman who cannot read; nevertheless,
she has been able to keep herself employed and "was never fired from a
job.... I used to clean house for white people and they was good to me,
and I was happy and enjoyed it. I worked in the school kitchen for a

whole year; no, I don't got no problems getting jobs." She also worked at housekeeping and in the kitchen at two different nursing homes for over five years even offering to work double shifts for those who wanted days off. Today, in order to have money and some independence, she sells health products and cosmetics, asking her customers to write up their own orders, does sewing, cleans houses, and does other odd jobs.

Self-educated, Maria has become quite competent at crossing the borders of language, culture, and community even if she is not always comfortable doing so. Limiting herself to familiar places, avoiding downtown with its numerous signs, creating a family life surrounded by her children, Maria may be invisible to many. The segregated barrios in larger cities conceal from the broader population the lives of the outsiders, and they have become for many Anglos just a place to get a good Mexican meal. Border crossings are something Maria has had to become adept at from an early age, like all Mexican Americans who live in two cultural worlds.

Patricia: The Responsibilities of Family

The whites were always treated better. Well it was only here in Colorado Springs. Back home [New Mexico] it wasn't like this, you know; as a matter of fact, there wasn't even a white teacher. They were all Mexican/Spanish-speaking teachers.

Even as far as the best uniforms 'cause we had to wear uniforms for P.E. The rest of us would just get the faded one and stuff like that. But I never thought that it was discrimination until—I still don't think it's discrimination. I think it's just you didn't put your foot down and go get it. We were just timid I feel.

Back then I didn't think about it. I knew I was in a lower class all through high school, and it was because of a lot of little things, like my language. I didn't understand it all. I would see what the whites were doing, and to me, I always wanted to be like them—smart.

I met with Patricia several times at the local community center where she brought her mother-in-law for luncheon meals twice a week. Sometimes we had only a few minutes to talk before her charge was ready to leave. Twice we scheduled our times so we could be more leisurely in our conversations. The community center was a busy place and predominately populated with Mexican Americans, although Anglo youth also would join in the basketball games after school.

Patricia worked in housekeeping at a local hospital but had to leave her position because of a back injury that left her unable to perform the necessary bending and lifting. She was collecting disability when I met her, and was studying on her own with some old workbooks she still had of her husband's in order to find another kind of work. "When I got my back injury I stopped working two jobs because I was working at the hospital and I would also do cleaning. I'd like to find a place that has on-the-job training, but I don't know where to look. I've just been thinking that I have to do something better, something for myself." She is married with two children, and her husband was working on getting a GED "because he can get transferred into management."

Patricia, thirty-five years old, was the oldest of nine children and grew up in Penasco, a Spanish community in the hills of northern New Mexico. She lived there with her mother, her siblings, and her extended family. Her father lived and worked in Colorado, returning home periodically and sending money every month for the family to live on. Patricia's grandparents were also from New Mexico and lived nearby. Although she claims they were afraid of the indigenous Indians, she says she is part Indian. It is not uncommon for Mexican Americans in northern New Mexico to claim their Spanish heritage over the intermarriages with the indigenous people of the region.

When her mother died, Patricia took on the responsibility of keeping her family together. "One teacher in New Mexico encouraged me when my mom died. 'You can keep your family together.' Everybody wanted to divide the children all over. We would have big old fights with grandma. But I stood my ground and I called my dad and said, 'Either you come and pick us up and take us with you or I'm taking all this stuff and we're gonna go there.'" Patricia moved with her sisters and brothers to Colorado to be with their father, and she took care of the family. "My sister and me, we kinda shared a lot of the work, but when my dad would get mad, I would get the whole load. My dad would hit me because I would get in front to protect the little ones."

As a fifteen-year-old, it was too difficult to manage her responsibilities and go to school at the same time. Even though most of her siblings got their high school diplomas, Patricia did not. "It was really hard for me, and then it was real hard raising kids and doing my work. I got them through school; some of them quit, but still they're in no trouble with the law. It was hard. I don't use it as an excuse like a lot of people use it. I had to do all this and it was something I did, and they turned out a little bit good."

When in school, Patricia had trouble with English; the other children would make fun of her English pronunciations. She also had trouble spelling. "I knew I wasn't up to where I should have been. I wasn't very smart in reading, writing, math, anything. I just glided through everything." Tracked into vocational courses, Patricia described her junior high years. She told me, "My spelling's really bad, but I took the basic math that's required. I took a lot of home and child development and that kind of stuff—sewing, a lot of that stuff 'cause I planned on being a homemaker." In recalling her failures with spelling, a major problem was that she didn't know what the spelling words meant. This extended into reading as well. "I didn't know what I was reading or writing, even if we looked the word up in the dictionary, we really couldn't pronounce the words correctly." When I asked Patricia about talking with her counselor about it, she laughed. "I wanted to be smart and I wanted to better myself, but I couldn't. I would pray that God would help me to concentrate on my spelling words and would get them all right. I just wasn't motivated to do it. I finally settled for what I could do. I'd never even seen my counselor; I really wasn't even school material."

Patricia's position in the family as eldest girl meant certain responsibilities for her that put multiple pressures on her, often at the expense of her own welfare, for example, her own education. While I have not directly examined gender issues in this study, it was apparent in several of the women's stories that gender roles played an important part in the course of their lives. For many Mexican American women, working outside the home is a cultural tradition rooted in colonial economic conditions of pastoral life where women not only took care of the home but maintained their own gardens and livestock thus contributing to the economic production of the family. Responding to contemporary times with its cash economy, cultural traditions persist in the form of juggling family and outside jobs. As a girl and young woman, Patricia took care of her siblings after her mother's death and also tried to go to school; as a wife, she contributes economically by working at the local hospital while maintaining her own family. For Patricia, education was a defining factor in what economic options were open to her.

Jose: Wanting Something Better

> When I was working, I didn't want to do this all my life, working hard and all that. I don't want to be all hurting when I'm old so I wanted to see if I could get a job that wasn't as hard. I had trouble reading a lot so I thought the only good job for me was probably hard labor work, but I don't think so no more. I think I should have just stayed in school and finished. Now I feel worried about getting some kind of training to get a better job.

Jose and I met at the Job Training Employment office in Denver, a noisy set of rooms partitioned off once you stepped off the elevator on the second floor of a sterile, and somewhat unkept, government building. I had arranged some quiet corner office space with a grey desk and two chairs to talk with people who fit the research criteria and who were willing to be interviewed. Jose, at first, was reluctant to talk with me, perhaps because I was white and female, perhaps because he was just unsure of what kinds of things I would ask him to talk about.

Jose was a small-framed man, shoulders slightly bent over. He had dark circles under his eyes and a leathered, brown face. His eyesight was poor, he said, and he had a back injury that kept him always searching for work that he could physically do. His hands and fingers were stained from years of hard physical labor and "cheap paying manual jobs, nothing that was going to get me anywhere," as he called them. At the age of fifty-two, he seemed older than his years. He was looking for work again when I met him, and he spent Mondays at the employment office hoping new listings would turn something up for him. After meeting with an employment counselor, he agreed to speak with me.

Vocational training in welding as a young adult got Jose work for several years until his accident when he slipped and fell on the concrete floor in the welding shop. He went through physical rehabilitation for awhile and then on to barber school. "They told me I should be able to stand without trouble, I just couldn't bend. It hurt too much, and I had to give up welding, but when I was in [barber] training, I found I couldn't stand except for short times so I never was a barber." While barbering didn't work out for Jose, he "tried all the programs, but I didn't qualify for training," hoping to develop other skills that might help him find a job that paid a living wage. "You can only do so much," he told me, "doin' the wrong things you don't qualify, living a clean life, don't qualify."

In recounting his days of schooling, Jose talked about his sense of being invisible to the teachers. "They didn't seem to care if I was there, they didn't notice whether or not I was having trouble." He left school half way through the tenth grade; he remarked about the teachers and students. "There were only three Mexicans in the school, me and my brothers, and one black. All the teachers were Anglo. I didn't feel I was getting as much as others. [The teachers] had an attitude thing, 'figure it out.' I can't push it all on prejudice, but it was there, and the teachers didn't care to help. There was no reason to stay." Jose left school, married at a young age, and has two daughters who have successfully graduated from the school Jose left many years earlier, although he says, "Teachers still have the same attitudes, and it put worry on me with my daughters." When I asked Jose the value of a high school diploma, he commented that, "The opportunities were not there after dropping out but no, it wouldn't help get me a better job. But I would be positioned better to feel good about myself."

Jose's ethnic and cultural background has provided both pain and joy. His great-grandparents moved up from Mexico to Las Vegas, New Mexico, where his parents met and married. When the family farmland was lost to debt, his family moved to the Denver area. Before settling into construction work, his father found work in various manual trades for short periods of time, moving from one job to another the first couple years. After moving to Denver, English became more and more important, although Jose's mother stressed the need for her children to learn English at an early age. She taught her children English at home. "Mom thought we should get in the flow and learn English—it would be easier for us. Anglos looked at us like, you're dumb because you should know English, but we felt we were dumb because we should know Spanish. Bilingual, I love it because I'm able to correspond with everybody."

Searching for an easier life, away from the backbreaking labor of manual work, Jose is a proud man who holds his cultural identity deep within himself; it seems to carry him through hard times of unemployment and experiences of educational exclusion. The Spanish language is a strong influence on his interactions with others and how he feels about himself. Jose is representative of the others who identify with their native language as a strength interwoven into the fabric of their lives.

The Struggle for Cultural Survival

The experiences of the five people described here illustrate some of the most important ideas I came to know about Mexican Americans, including notions of difference, people searching for their place and trying to live in two cultures, while wanting something better for themselves and their families. Gonzales's (1972) epic poem, I am Joaquin, quoted in part at the beginning of this chapter, goes on to say:

> My fathers have lost the economic battle and won the struggle of cultural survival. And now! I must choose between the paradox of the victory of the spirit, despite physical hunger, or to exist in the grasp of American social neurosis, sterilization of the soul and a full stomach. (P. 8-9)

Maria, Jose, Carlos, Patricia, Olivia, and the others who told their stories are confronted with this dilemma of which Gonzales speaks. Cultural survival, in the midst of a society that insists on weaving all the colors of the rainbow into one piece of cloth, mixing different fruit in a bowl, and melting all distinguishing features of multiple cultures into one, is a survival that is built upon solidarity and daily threats. For Mexican Americans of the Southwest, it may seem easier because there are more Mexican Americans there than in other parts of the country. Don't be fooled by the numbers; politically they are less visible than their population would indicate. Colorado, among others, is an English-only state, a racist response to the threat of a growing Spanish-speaking population within the state. Yet, Mexican Americans do survive and even thrive according to their own ideas, their own values, their own cultural ways. They are fully engaged in their communities and neighborhoods while responding to exploitation at every turn.

Chapter 3
Tensions of Colonization, Culture, and Difference

> In telling and retelling of their stories, they create communities of memory. (Takaki 1993, 14)

As people share knowledge of their worlds including the everyday routines, habits, social interactions, and values, they do so from an historically positioned vantage point. Ascriptive categories of race, ethnicity, class, and gender define and confound one's position within socially constructed realities. Likewise, culture as both an institution rooted in family, schools, media, and other structures, and as a set of coping tools and strategies, influences and promotes meaning in the everyday dealings of social life. Hall (1992) reminds us that "we all speak from a particular place, out of a particular history, out of a particular experience, out of a particular culture, without being contained by that position" (258), while Clifford (1986) talks of cultural poetics as an interplay of voices, of positioned utterances, contested, temporal and emergent. Further, all cultural voices are multisubjective, contingent, power-laden, incongruent, and offer political solutions to everyday ne-gotiated realities. Williams (1981) directs us to the ideological aspects of culture as a series of sign systems and social practices formed through formal and conscious beliefs for the purpose of social and cultural re-production. Competing sets of ethics are visible between dominant and nondominant groups, but also exist among, and within, various cultural groups. The majority of people in the United States being people of color, women, and the working class, are continuously moving back and forth across cultural borders.

As a people who live in the light of their own history in the United States, how have Mexican Americans organized the world and the meanings they attach to what goes on in the world? There is no univer-sal response or reality for Mexican Americans who live in the South-west. Yet, moving back and forth across cultural borders, Mexican Americans interface with the contemporary power structure of main-stream society and its dominant values of Eurocentric individualism, competition, superiority, and middle-class privilege. As they do so, they create a set of multicultural and multivaried experiences that influence and create a politics of identity and culture dependent upon everyday practices and discourses. Our identities are crucial to our subjective sense of who we are and who we can become. As people traverse boundaries into the public sphere of daily experience, a process of nego-tiation takes place as a result of discontinuities, contradictions, and oppositions rather than continuities and coincidence between social contexts and individuals.

The men and women who participated in this study have ancestors from old Mexico and parts of the old northern frontier of Mexico that were incorporated into the United States after the Mexican conquest, specifically, New Mexico, southern Colorado, and Texas. Thus, they are descendants of people indigenous to the region. While there are many historical accounts of United States imperialism and colonialism in the Southwest that do not need to be repeated here, there is a need to provide a historical backdrop against which to examine contempo-rary educational patterns. By focusing on historical constructions of group identity, we get a clearer picture of how Mexican Americans might make sense of their cultural identities and how to interpret indi-vidual responses. People are bound to their history, both collectively and individually.

There have been many defining historical events that have influenced Mexican Americans' identity formation and reformation. Several significant and widely discussed historical events include the 1848 Treaty of Guadalupe Hidalgo, the loss of Mexican and Spanish land and land grants, and the continuous cycle of first recruiting and then expelling of Mexican labor into the United Sates. Taking a long view into the past and linking it to the present and potentially to the future might suggest a linear process, but that is not the scenario that I intend to illuminate. Rather we must take a more holistic and dynamic view, which continually weaves and draws in connecting threads of experience. Situating such a historical grounding requires a critical understanding of individual and collective memory such as the historical conditioning of colonization and exclusion deeply embedded in cultural, racial, and ethnic norms, values, sanctions, processes, and relationships.

Colonization of the Southwest

The Mexican people and their culture have had a continuous presence in the Southwest for the past four hundred years. This fact alone distinguishes this section of United States history and the people who live in the region. California and the southwestern section of the United States, including Texas, New Mexico, parts of what is now Arizona, the southern half of Colorado, Utah, and Nevada, once belonged to the great empire of Mexico.

Under the 1848 Treaty of Guadalupe Hidalgo, Mexico lost almost half of its land mass to the United States in a two-year battle precipitated by the annexation of Texas in 1845. Texas, New Mexico, and California had been sparsely populated regions; the Spanish had difficulty convincing people to move into these territories and settle there to secure its holdings. As the westward movement of the United States progressed, Anglos began settling into the Texas and California territories of Mexico. In fact, Mexico gave land grants to non-Mexicans who agreed to settle in order to populate the area. As a result, Texas was settled more thoroughly with Anglos than other areas of northern Mexico. Mexico took action. Outlawing slavery, a system which the Anglos used to advance cultivation of the land, and prohibiting further American immigration into Texas, Mexico closed the border. Furious at these restrictions, Americans continued to cross the border as illegal aliens. Struggling for almost ten years to take over this territory, the United States annexed Texas in 1846. This led Mexico to cease relations with the United States. A United States emissary was sent to Mexico to settle the Texas matter and attempt to purchase the areas of California and New Mexico as well. There was an outbreak of hostilities between Mexican and American troops along the Rio Grande River, where American troops blockaded the mouth of the river. This in itself was an act of war. Claiming that Mexico, however, had invaded the United States territory and attacked American forces, the United States declared war on Mexico in 1846.

Having gained its independence from Spain, Mexico was still a young republic of just twenty-five years at that time, and was trying to define its nationhood and governmental structures in the late 1800s. As a poor country, it was almost in ruins. Kanellos (1998) recounts a news article from *The American Whig Review* that summarizes what led President James Polk and the United States into the Mexican-American War and its victory. "What could she do....We are Anglo-Saxon Americans; it is our destiny to possess and to rule this continent;...we are a chosen people, and this was our allotted inheritance, and we must drive out all nations before us!" (76-77).

With the signing of the Treaty of Guadalupe Hidalgo, the Mexican nationals were given one year to choose citizenship. Under the treaty's terms people could choose to become citizens of the United States or retain their Mexican citizenship. In either case, their property, religious, and civil rights were to be protected. Mexico sent commissioners to New Mexico, Texas, and California to assist families in moving back to Mexico, offering land and equipment to those willing to repatriate. But only three thousand chose to leave their lands, and in later repatriation efforts, only two thousand more Mexicans moved to Mexico; seventy-five thousand Mexicans remained in the United States by conquest. Little did the newly conquered know that later their rights would not be recognized nor would they be able to enjoy the freedoms of the northern frontier.

The expansion of the United States into the Southwest is explained by many as part of the Manifest Destiny of Anglo America. Manifest Destiny was essentially a manipulated appeal and an attempt to secure broad popular support for an expansionist policy of particular benefit to certain political and economic interests. Politicians and writers who espoused Manifest Destiny and the superiority of the white race along with President Polk included Thomas Jefferson, Benjamin Franklin, and Ralph Waldo Emerson who observed that the economic ends justified the means. Mexican diplomat Manuel Crescion Rejon predicted that "descendants of the Indians that we are, the North Americans hate us, their spokesmen deprecate us, even if they recognize the justice of our cause, and they consider us unworthy to form with them one nation and one society, they clearly manifest that their future expansion begins with the territory that they take from us and pushing aside our citizens who inhabit the land" (Takaki 1993, 177-178).

As a minority, Mexican Americans were politically vulnerable and powerless. Anglo-only democracy prevailed through laws aimed at Mexicans such as an antivagrancy act, which described vagrants as those of Spanish or Indian blood. The mounting racism that originally justified Anglo expansion as Manifest Destiny also extended to the use of the Spanish language and the culture of the Spanish speakers. There was a strong United States resistance to extending citizenship to other races, and the question of whether the states should come in as "free" or "slave" states was at issue. Indeed, the numerical majority of Mexicans in New Mexico caused the area to remain a territory rather than gain statehood like Texas and California where there were many more Anglos. New Mexico was continuously denied statehood until 1912; Colorado became a state in 1918. Opposition to New Mexico's statehood was voiced by many. It was believed that the Mexicans had failed because they were a mixed, inferior race with considerable Indian and some black blood; and stereotypes of Mexicans solidified. Derogatory terms such as greaser, lazy, cruel, cowardly, and shiftless were used to describe the new Americans and quickly preceded the expropriation of their lands. Denigration of the Mexican American peoples was used in order to justify settlement and exploitation by the Anglo Americans and further the doctrine of Manifest Destiny.

Although differences emerged among the regional histories of California, Texas, New Mexico, Colorado, and the other Southwestern states due to geography, themes of lost land grants, having to work for Anglo Americans, and displacement were common. The United States disregarded the provisions of the treaty. Mexicans Americans and their property were at the mercy of political, economic, and legal systems that were completely foreign to them. As land-hungry Anglo pioneers and entrepreneurs moved into the Southwest, the Mexican Americans fell victim to legal manipulations, fraud, and outright theft. Using the United States legal system, savvy Anglo Americans with money and connections were able to challenge Mexican American-held land grants. Public notices of efforts to collect debts listed in the English language newspapers was a tactic often used to begin the process of acquiring land from the Spanish-speaking Mexican Americans. Unfamiliar with the legal system, and having insufficient resources to fund legal cases, Mexican Americans lost their land and homes.

In the New Mexico region, the Sangre de Cristo land grant, issued in 1844, originally encompassed approximately one million acres covering all of New Mexico, southern Colorado, and parts of Texas. In addition to the Sangre de Cristo land grant, the Conejos, Vigil St. Vrain, Nolan, Tierra Amarilla, and the Baca land grants covered over eight million acres in southern Colorado (De Baca, 1998). The northern part of New Mexico and the San Luis Valley in southern Colorado were characterized by planned "communal" villages with open community spaces for grazing. A multicultural farming system provided a sustainable lifestyle and ecology in this region by supplying each community with "access to most of the life zones in the locality. Anglo Americans, coming from the east to settle in this region, adopted the square-grid topography of the 1785 ordinance. A national land survey program based on the township-and-range system divided the country into a rigid grid of square parcels one mile on a side, subdivided into quarter sections of 160 acres" (Pena 1998, 251-252). The land-use pattern homogenized the natural and cultural landscapes that were considered obstacles to "mechanized economies-of-scale favored by Anglo Americans" (252) and contributed to the Mexican American's difficulties in sustaining ranches and farms.

Regional and local government activities also influenced land grant outcomes through the imposition of manipulated fixed land-taxes, a major factor in dispossessing the former landowners, thus keeping with the requirements of capitalist agricultural development. Fixed land-taxes, specific to this region, was a significant mechanism by which the transfer of land took place. Under the Mexican system, taxes were levied on the products of the land rather than the land itself. In an area where production varied from year to year, a fixed land-tax placed a heavy burden on the ranchers and farmers. The Mexican American subsistence farmer living in villages was singularly unprepared to adjust to a fixed land-tax system. By the 1930s, Anglos came to own four-fifths of the former land grant areas. This was a major loss to the economic viability of the villages. The struggle over land grant rights in this area of northern New Mexico and southern Colorado continues to this day. Mexican Americans are fighting for their rights to land deeded to ancestors decades ago, now owned by Anglo ranchers who adhere to sole proprietorship and require vast expanses for grazing cattle. In other cases, Mexican Americans have been able to hold on to their land but fear that their neighbors, who sell off land to developers, are breaking up the communal grazing grounds. Recently in northern New Mexico, a man was asked to put up his land grant sections as collateral that was three times greater than the loan he requested so that he could invest in more livestock.

The power of the state in the displacement of people and colonization of the Southwest cannot be overlooked. The Court of Private Land Claims, set up in New Mexico in 1891 and elsewhere in the Southwest and California in the late nineteenth century, are examples of state powers affecting Mexican Americans that expropriated land, formally and informally, after the conquest and well into the twentieth century. The procedures placed the burden of proof on the claimants, but more importantly, factors such as the language of the courts, the application of Anglo legal precepts to grants made under a different legal system, and the location of federal land offices seriously biased the outcomes against the original claimants, particularly the Mexican Americans. "By letting a major part of the burden of dispossession fall on such a seemingly impartial institutional mechanism, the facade of state neutrality could be more easily maintained while still obtaining the desired result in the end" (Barrera 1979, 166). In facilitating the transfer of land, the state acted not only on behalf of capitalist class interests but on its own behalf. A great deal of the land that was taken over in New Mexico went directly into the public domain. The state is an institution with its own interests that often coincide with those of the dominant class.

Another factor that fueled displacement was the move from an exchange economy to a cash economy. The Mexican American exchange economy was characterized by an ethic of communal assistance whereby people helped each other whenever needed, a livelihood based on bartering of goods and services, and commitment to community engagement and culture. Even in hard times, people could rely on the communal system of responsibility (Deutsch 1987). This meant families could remain together and survival was ensured. Losing their land, however, meant that people were unable to farm, raise livestock, and participate in the communal exchange economy. The loss of land coupled with the new cash economy forced many to look outside of their communities for work and sustenance. Thus, they were both dispossessed of land and alienated on their native soil.

As Mexican Americans moved from landowners to laborers they were relegated to the worst jobs in every labor sector. In the sugar beet and cotton fields, they were employed as stoop labor; on the railroads they replaced the Chinese and were sent wherever they were needed; and in the mines, they carried two hundred pound packs strapped to head and shoulders. They were forced to live in company towns and encouraged to purchase goods on credit that chained them to the company. Often what began as a strategy of survival, namely migration to where the jobs were for specific periods of time followed by returning home during winter months, turned into a lifestyle of dependence and subordination.

During the early 1900s, Mexican immigrants, mostly from the agricultural labor class, crossed the border into the United States. The greatest surge occurred during the 1920s, when almost half a million Mexicans arrived. The influx of Mexican labor into the United States served to meld, in the Anglo mind, the kinship between Mexicans and Mexican Americans. At various times, this had differing effects on the Mexican Americans. In the early days of recruiting Mexicans into the United States, the Mexican Americans joined in solidarity with the Mexicans against unjust working conditions, yet at other times, United States economic conditions served to put them at odds with one another. More recently, working-class Mexican Americans are threatened by the Mexicans who might take their jobs.

Immigrants joined the Mexican Americans in the segmented labor market where both were assigned not only the worst jobs but received the lowest pay; a two-tiered wage labor market had developed with Anglos making more than the Mexicans and Mexican Americans for the same work. Low-wage Mexican and Mexican American labor helped to drive down wages generally, and they were often called in as a strategy to prevent strikes.

The labor situation for Mexican Americans deteriorated over time as they found themselves part of a caste labor system. They believed they deserved better working conditions, higher pay and respect, and they went out on strike many times in various parts of the Southwest. For example, in Colorado in the early 1900s, Mexican American coal miners working for Rockefeller's Colorado Fuel and Iron Company struck for an eight-hour day, abolition of pay in company scrip, a better supply of pure air as prescribed by state law, semimonthly pay, the right to trade in any store, the right to choose any boarding place and doctor, and enforcement of existing mining laws. Undergirding the 1913-1914 strike was the right of union membership and representation. Although the United Mine Workers of America lost the strike, the viciousness of the struggle aroused unprecedented public reaction and much needed attention to their plight (Vallejo 1998).

In the sugar beet fields, Mexican Americans found the work to be one of the most disagreeable of all agricultural occupations. The living conditions in labor camps were demoralizing and inhumane, and growers felt no responsibility to the laborers. One of the most powerful strikes of farm workers occurred in 1933 in California when twelve thousand workers resisted wage reductions. In breaking the strike, employers evicted the laborers and dumped their belongings on the highway. Local police arrested strikers and condemned the workers as trash. In the end, the workers won a compromise wage rate.

The strikes reflected a Mexican ethnic solidarity against the Anglo bosses. Everywhere in the barrios, there were benevolent associations that supported the strikes. Members were laborers as well as professionals, women as well as men. They helped cover medical and funeral expenses, provided loans, and raised money in dire times. Through these organizations, Mexican Americans resisted exploitation and racism, maintained a strong cultural attachment to their ethnic roots, and were determined to claim their rights and dignity in "occupied" Mexico.

However, Mexican Americans remained at the bottom of the socioeconomic ladder even though they had attained full employment during World War II. In response to the loss of hundreds of thousands of Mexican American farm workers, who were either drafted or enlisted in service to the country, the Bracero Program was begun in 1942. The

Bracero Program brought Mexicans into the country and by 1960 they comprised a quarter of the farm labor. The Mexicans were treated even more poorly than the Mexican Americans. As a result, wages were lowered and often became the norm for agricultural workers. Abuse and discrimination against the Mexicans produced extremely poor housing, excessive charges, unauthorized deductions, and poor working conditions. The Mexican Americans opposed the program because it took jobs away from them, and some worked diligently for the deportation of the Mexicans. Well-known Mexican American human rights, social, and church groups protested the Bracero Program. This created bitterness between the two groups, but the common language, history, and culture helped to develop close social ties.

"The repatriations of almost a million Mexican undocumented immigrants in the 1950s, even while applauded by many middle-class Mexican American organizations, created tragic disruptions in family life and damaged the Mexican American enclave economy that depended on immigrant paychecks. Most of the labor contractors who managed the Bracero Program and recruited Mexican farm workers were bilingual Americanized Mexican Americans" (De Baca 1998). Other Mexican Americans, especially those in the working class, felt threatened by the newly arrived Mexican laborers. The Bracero Program was discontinued in 1965 with an agreement by both countries that Mexicans would be employed in the factories, or maquiladoras, that United States corporations would build in Mexico.

During the 1950s, the majority of employed Mexican Americans were blue-collar workers who had moved into the barrios of bigger cities and metropolitan areas as agricultural work became mechanized. There was noticeable movement into Denver where the construction industry needed more and more laborers to facilitate the economic boom. The greatest shift in lifestyle came for those from New Mexico who left traditional rural villages and moved to the big cities of Colorado and California. Not only did they have little financial or job security, but they had to either compete with, or forge alliances with, other ethnic groups who were new migrants. They had to adjust to a changing industrial economy and had little time to engage in opposing the discrimination they were now finding in the cities.

The essence of the colonial system exists first in the economic realm through a subordinate labor force, but extends into political institutions, the educational system, and all social structures within society. Schooling in the Southwest varied across the states, of course, but it is safe to say that the goal of education for Mexican Americans was to prepare them for their place in the labor market; the fields of sugar beets and cotton, the floors of the factories, and the manual building trades of expansion. The primary function of the schools from earliest days onward has been to Americanize their culture and to mute their language. Whereas segregated English-speaking schools were the primary model of schooling for Mexican American children in the Southwest justified on the grounds of their unique needs, in New Mexico and southern Colorado, due in large part to the numerical majority of Mexican Americans, children attended separate schools where Spanish was spoken and the teachers, for the most part, were Mexican Americans. In southern Colorado and in some areas of New Mexico, it was not uncommon for children to go without formal schooling due to the limited number of facilities and resources. According to some, religious schools, in particular the Presbyterian mission schools, were the surest route to an education for many Mexican American children. As more Anglos moved to southern Colorado after 1950, the political control of Mexican Americans diminished even more, and with it, control over the schools.

Mexican American families who migrated to northern Colorado found integrated schools in the larger cities, but these institutions often had separate classes for Mexican Americans where their Spanish was ridiculed and their culture attacked. This separation was based on Anglo attitudes of racial inferiority toward Mexican Americans. Children were trained to become obedient, compliant workers, and school policy was influenced by the needs of the local economies. Middle-class Mexican Americans, however, expected eventual synthesis and coexistence in the dominant culture, partly due to their participation in war efforts and partly because they believed in the American dream. They were especially distressed by the segregation of public facilities such as the schools.

Political action groups, such as the G.I. Forum and the League of United Latin American Citizens (LULAC), opposed discrimination and worked to form alliances across the Southwest while working on local political issues. Political involvement has been a strong tradition of Mexican Americans as they have struggled for their rights, whether

over land ownership, working conditions in the fields, mines or factories, or segregation in the schools. For the most, part these political efforts were dominated by liberals and conservatives. But during the
1960s, the Chicano Movement, a radical response to segregation, dominated the scene. It attempted to redefine the political, social, and cultural status of Mexican-descent people, Mexican Americans and Mexicans alike. Led by radicals in Texas, Colorado, and California, they
advocated cultural and political self-determination. They wanted to
move beyond assimilation to integration by retaining or reclaiming
their language, culture, and pride in their Mexican heritage.

Conditions have changed over the years for Mexican Americans,
but as a group, they still provide the largest proportion of migrant labor,
and are represented heavily in the grueling labor of meat packing, do-
mestic work, construction, factory, and other blue-collar labor. They
have a significantly higher concentration in low-income jobs, higher
unemployment, and a median income that is approximately 70 percent
that of Anglos (Feagin 1991). Displacement, cultural and economic
subordination, discrimination, marginality, and even internal colonization are a part of many lives. From the earliest days, Mexican "Otherness" was constructed by the dominant society. "The persistence of ra-
cial/ethnic inequality in this society is the result of th[e] historic
[colonial] relationship which continues to operate today" (Barrera
1979, 197).

Counter to those who argue for full Latino/a assimilation to the
colonization process (Chavez 1991), critical theorists call for continued
resistance and reaffirmation to sustain indigenous cultures. Most of the
Southwest's cultures only gradually developed a resistance to colonization as the dreams and promises of economic, social, and political opportunities were not fulfilled (Sibley 1992). The harshness that historically characterized the Mexican American situation has lessened to
some degree, but a backlash against their demands and reemergence of
marginality is evident.

Familial Histories

Men and women in this study recalled how their parents, grandparents, or great-grandparents had moved north from Mexico to New
Mexico to Colorado. This continuous movement also included

migration from southern Colorado, particularly through the San Luis Valley, on up to Colorado Springs, Denver, or Greeley where they worked in the sugar beet fields, on the railroads, in the coal mines, and in the factories.

> My grandmother moved up to New Mexico before my mother was born. She (my mother) was born in Questa (New Mexico). My father's from Alamosa (Colorado). They met in Denver. My father worked in the fields before he moved here. Then he worked on the railroad. He started working when he was eleven years old. (Gloria)

> We were raised in just a little town of Spanish-speaking people, it's a little town in New Mexico. My father lived here [Colorado], this is where he's lived really for all his work and my mom and us stayed back in New Mexico. He would come back and leave again and send her $20.00 a month. (Patricia)

As a result of the migration of families and family members, a regional community of Mexican Americans stretched across New Mexico and Colorado linked by kinship networks and expanded by a strategy of economic survival. Migration had become an essential and integral part of life for Mexican American villagers.

Before the Mexican Americans began working in the beet fields, Great Western Sugar Company had brought German Russians in from Nebraska who had experience in the beet producing areas. Before long they were becoming tenant farmers and landowners themselves. By 1916 Great Western Sugar was recruiting field laborers to replace the German Russians by advertising in local newspapers, on the radio, and even calling door-to-door in southern Colorado, New Mexico, and Texas. Mexican Americans filled the need for beet workers (Aguayo 1998). Sandra tells of her family's migration to the beet fields.

> My grandma was born here in Colorado, and my grandfather, this was on my mom's side, was born in Texas. Now their parents were born in Mexico. Some of my grandma's brothers and sisters were born in Mexico and then the youngest of them were born here. So like my grandma was one of the youngest. She was born here in the United States. They were farmers, worked in the fields in Fort Morgan. My mom did the beets and the onions and all that stuff. My dad was raised in the colonies outside of Fort Morgan. They worked the fields too.

Maria related a series of moves they had to make in order for her father to find work to support his family. Her grandparents had owned pastoral land in central New Mexico but had lost the title to Anglos due to debt incurred. Her father worked on the railroad in eastern New Mexico for a time. He moved the family into town after losing the railroad job, but there was no work there. Without work, nor prospects of work, the family was ready to go wherever they had to in order to find economic stability. Listening to the radio one morning, Maria's father heard the advertising that Great Western Sugar was using to recruit workers for its sugar beet farms in Colorado. "All farms in Colorado were putting ads on the radio. They needed people to come and work in the fields, beets, sugar beets," according to Maria. "My daddy had to. We would just move the family and they had a house for us."

Responding to the recruitment efforts of Great Western Sugar, Maria's family history documents the pattern of economic migration that led from homesteading to entering the wage labor economy. The types of work that brought people north were seasonal wage labor jobs, which were used by Mexican Americans to maintain cultural autonomy, provide multisource income, and maintain relations of community with villagers in New Mexico. Strategies of migration and regional communities helped to define and sustain not only economic, but also cultural autonomy (Deutsch 1987).

Great Western Sugar Company subsidized clusters of homes in Colorado for the Mexican American farm workers; they issued materials to laborers on credit against earnings from the next growing season in Greeley, Loveland, Fort Collins, Brighton, Ovid, Brush, Hudson, Fort Morgan, and Kersey. The housing clusters were isolated and always a distance from the nearest Anglo community, usually located out of sight. These clusters became the colonias of Colorado that created ethnic and cultural separation as well as distinct economic districts. Most were viewed by the Anglos as an "appropriate means of keeping the Mexicans together. Even Spanish American families, who managed to edge into the fringe of the white communities, sometimes looked down at their compatriots living in the colonias" (Aguayo 1998, 115).

The individuals I talked to continued in the traditional employment areas of manual labor open to Mexican Americans such as gardening, building maintenance, construction, factory work, and health care. Several worked in office situations, one owned a grocery store in a

Chicano community, and several were unemployed. A small number of individuals were collecting welfare when I met them. All people lived in one of the Mexican American communities in either Denver or Colorado Springs. These are neighborhoods of mixed economic and racial groups. There is a heterogeneity of community conditions where people lived including neatly kept houses and yards with safe parks, churches, and thriving businesses. A few people owned their own homes. Some respondents lived, however, in public housing projects where community conditions included boarded up buildings, dirt yards, and empty lots. In both urban communities, there are segregated neighborhoods, inter and intraracial gang rivalries, limited political and cultural visibility of Latino/a groups, inadequately protected neighborhoods, underfunded inner-city schools, and ethnic and racial housing projects.

Historic and contemporary subjectivity converge. As people remember and recount the details of familial migrations due to the loss of land and livelihood, they position themselves within the collective history of United States Mexican Americans.

Politics of Cultural Identity and Difference

The collective history of Mexican Americans, one of colonization and forced assimilation, is one basis for trying to understand how people make sense of their world. Contemporary life is shaped by hegemonic ideologies of white superiority. How Chicanos/as respond to myths of democracy, freedom, equality, and individualism, and the relationship between the past and present strongly influence sense of self and place in the world.

People's social cultural identities are formed and reformed through everyday lived experiences grounded in the past. This is an important point, for identity is a social construction that relies on continuous social interactions and social ideologies of what is possible. Beliefs about oneself as part of a social cultural group is but one ingredient; how one is perceived and treated by others and the status the group has achieved all play into how group identity is formed. An important dynamic of continual reformation is also at play. People not only bring their pasts with them, experiences that shape contemporary perspectives and a sense of who one is, but identity is continually reformed in each present-day encounter with family members, friends, and strangers alike.

Cultural identity is constantly negotiated through social policies such as schooling and housing, and through political and economic struggles of differing interests. The dynamic nature of identity creates a space within which change is possible, a space where struggle can take place. As people respond and adjust to shifting environments and interactions, they do so from contextual specificity, yet each individual responds differently.

An identity of difference and displacement questions subjectivity and power, where border crossings and marginality are interwoven into the construction of knowledge; a knowledge that is always partial and positional. A state of belonging or not belonging based on discontinuities with the dominant culture, material conditions of class, and subordination at every turn creates oppositional discourses of subjugated knowledges, "a whole set of knowledges that have been disqualified,...a differential knowledge incapable of unanimity and which owes its force only to the harshness with which it is opposed by everything surrounding it" (Foucault 1972, 41).

Cecilia's assessment of differences between Mexican Americans and Anglos reflects the underlying conflict as she sees it. She described an incident her nephew experienced as he searched for a construction job.

> One guy hiring my nephew—my nephew knew how to do the work but he didn't have the tools, and they said, "All you Mexicans, you never save your money and do what's right." They hired a white guy and they threw [my nephew] out. It's basically, they don't think we're intelligent enough to do things.

Cecilia went on:

> Spanish people are real hard workers. Anglos, I don't think, are too much into work. You see a lot of them not working [at manual labor]. I don't know if it's because of their education or whatever reason, you don't see a whole lot of them working and yet, you see the Spanish people really working hard. They're doing the [physical] jobs; maybe, Anglos just want something better.

Maria reported experiences of job discrimination throughout her life. As a young woman, she was taken advantage of by other nursing home employees. They would have Maria cover for them by having her punch their time cards in, yet she would do the work. Later, she'd clock them out. As a housekeeper, she was paid less than the nurses she covered for, and they took advantage of the situation by paying her the housekeeping rate and keeping the rest for themselves. In another incident, she reported filing a complaint against a boss for slander while employed at a restaurant. According to Maria, her boss threatened a fellow employee who was a witness to the incident with loss of the employee's job if she testified against him. With no one to testify on her behalf, Maria lost the case and had to repay a year's worth of unemployment she had collected.

Patricia told of a situation when she was a housekeeper in a hospital. She wanted to learn new skills so she could get a better job at the hospital but had trouble getting the support and assistance from her supervisor.

> When I asked them if I could take off a half-hour early to go to a medical terminology thing, they said no. I went and talked to the lady and said I could go on my days off because they won't let me take off a half-hour. But then she went and she talked to them and they arranged that I could take the half-hour. But I had to go clock out. What was so hard about the supervisor bending a little bit because a minority person wanted to get ahead?

Ruben talked about his struggles to find work that would pay him enough on which to live. "I was making $2.90 an hour at this bakery. I used to work double shifts, double lines to make enough money to get by." At another time he tried selling things from his truck. "I needed to do something. I could not stay home doing nothing. I have a wife and kids. We could not go to no welfare office looking for aid, that we could not do. Every morning I was out with my truck. I sold a lot of things. The only problem was the police. 'Show me the papers' they would say. I had no papers. The police took things from my truck, I would lose right there $20-$25 dollars or more all the time. I had no choice. That used to irritate me really bad."

Jose's experiences in securing jobs without a high school diploma were difficult and frustrating to him. In reflecting on whether a diploma would really help him to get good jobs, he stated that "most employers like to give the jobs to Anglos first." Eduardo took a different route. "I decided to open my own business, a grocery store, instead of working for other bosses. I like to support the Latino community here instead of helping the Anglos. I work here [in this neighborhood]. I shop here. This is where I live."

Another type of economic discrimination was identified for me by Norma.

> My landlord is very rich. Last year he put in the market the house where we live. He said he needed to sell it because of taxes. My husband wanted to buy it. They asked us $120,000 for the house. My husband offered him $100,000. The landlord said no. Three months later the new owner came to introduce himself. We could not believe that he was able to buy the house for only $90,000.

Yet economic discrimination is not the only difference with which individuals must contend. Community neglect was highlighted by several people. Reuben told me he did not feel his neighborhood was kept up "compared to all the other places that are around. There is always trash that blows around the streets and alleys." Norma, who lived in an old barrio in Denver, which is now integrated with African Americans, Asians, and Anglos, reflected on a similar situation in her neighborhood, but thought it was getting better. Olivia talked of her surprise at the differences between her neighborhood and a predominately Anglo suburban area. Her husband, who worked for the park department, took her to see a park project on which he had been working. She questioned him, "How come they have one like that and we don't? Where are we at?" The stark differences between the barrio neighborhoods and white, middle-class neighborhoods in Denver and Colorado Springs are cause for comparison. Pointing out the differences seems reasonable since these people are paying taxes for services, which they do not get.

Police protection, or lack thereof, was identified as another indication of the social and economic inequalities of everyday life. Juanita told me of an incident in her neighborhood.

> Just like the incident with this gal here. She liked to have parties, and they were really destroying her place, and they were fighting amongst each other. I don't know how many times the cops came out, and it was always the same excuse. Well, you know, until there's really something that you can see—in other words, what they were saying was until they actually hit

you and bruise you and shoot you, then we can come out and
do something about it.

Her story is not unique, unfortunately. Manuel and Roberto also related similar situations to me when they spoke about specific incidents
in their neighborhoods.

So we called the cops because it was getting out of hand and
we needed to have them come out, and I think it took them
probably over an hour to get there. I thought, these men
could be dead and they're barely getting there. It was unreal.
We had already taken care of it ourselves. And if something
would have happened someplace else, I think, they would
have been there a lot faster. (Manuel)

They're telling people there's really nothing we can do. We
only had one or two complaints from you. They want to see
the actual murder. They want to see the whole thing happen,
then, maybe they got something. (Roberto)

Community neglect by the police is indicative of the general disregard for people who live outside the mainstream. Lack of police protection, neglect of community services, and job discrimination are further
dimensions of the social differentials in these cities. Jose reminds us
that "we must stop the separateness. If we look at color, we have problems. There is really no one superior," at least in his mind.

The similarities between past and present oppression and differences experienced by Mexican Americans can be clearly seen. Awareness of group-based discrimination increases the longer people continue to be labeled, categorized, and discriminated against (Hurtado,
Gurin and Peng 1994). Moving back and forth between the dominant
culture and their ethnic culture, Mexican Americans must develop
fluid and multiple identities. This shifting consciousness allows one to
perceive simultaneously multiple social realities (Moraga and Anzaldua
1981; Anzaldua 1987). Crossing borders (cultural, political, and structural) generates physical, psychological, and spiritual tensions that,
over time, may become familiar, yet never comfortable. However, because Mexican Americans are positioned to live in the borders, shad-
ows, and margins, they become adept at keeping intact their shifting
and multiple identities and integrity. This is similar to the dual African
American identity, which is developed in order to survive in the white
world. A mask to seem other then who you are hides the true self from

the oppressor who would deny, crush, smother, or obliterate that which is the true identity.

Part of the politics of living such fluid multiplicity is the moving back and forth between externally imposed constructs of what it means to be Mexican American in today's society and internal, emergent understandings constructed from everyday experiences (Sparks 1993; Sparks and MacDaniels 1999). The social cultural identity is built upon the relationship between the individual and those around her or him with all the layers of understandings, experiences, and expectations of each coming into play. The inherent shifts and contradictions become visible when people tell their stories.

Communities of Assistance

Similarly, the ethic of care evidenced through the benevolent societies of the Southwest during the earlier twentieth century is preserved and played out within contemporary times. Communities of assistance, whereby people help each other, watch over each other, contribute and share their resources, have become traditional cultural mechanisms through which memories of a shared past are kept alive and where the dual identity mask can be set aside.

Ana relates her early years of taking care of her many brothers and sisters "protecting them, cleaning them, watching after them, and sending them to school." Her siblings depended on her to be there and take care of them. Likewise, recall Patricia and her sister who took care of the younger children in the family after their mother died. Patricia's father worked in Colorado Springs, while the family lived in a pastoral mountain town in northern New Mexico. Initially, friends and relatives, in efforts to help the family, wanted to split the children among them. Patricia dropped out of school because it was hard on her and she was responsible for the other children. Her father's insistence on her keeping up with her studies and her determination to keep the family together finally convinced family and friends to help her out rather than split the children among them. Eventually the children joined their father in Colorado.

During the days of working in the fields, all able family members had to contribute to the family coffers due to the low wages of manual labor and the high prices for commodities. Olivia told me of her disdain for field work and, as a teen, she convinced her mother to let her find an inside job so she wouldn't have to work the fields. She found a job at the local laundromat and "really loved that job." At the time her mother remarried; there were already four children, and the "strong headed" mother insisted on her children making financial and nonfinancial contributions to the family since the stepfather had acquired several individuals in the marriage package.

Meeting family responsibilities was not only felt by the women, but men talked of contributing as well as meeting obligations. Carlos, a young man in his late twenties, related his efforts to help his mother after she divorced. He knew he had caused her a lot of grief when he left school, but he tried to make it easier on her by contributing financially to the family. Eduardo talked of his dual role of father and student. He ended up leaving school because he "had a daughter to support" and had a hard time juggling both. He wasn't getting the kind of attention he felt he needed at school anyway. As he reflected on the difficulty he had of finding anything more than low-skill, grueling manual jobs, he was insistent that his two daughters finish school.

Another strong theme expressed was that of "not living off of others." Jose expressed dismay at falling between the cracks if one is just "down and out" and needs assistance to get back on your feet while Cecilia's comments reflected her view about getting assistance through welfare or public assistance. This presents a dilemma for those who have only their wage labor to count on, and the labor they most often get is low-paying manual labor.

> You can only do so much, but you can also be stopped there. I tried all the programs, but I didn't qualify. If you live a clean life you don't qualify. If a person's doing the wrong things you qualify. (Jose)

> It's like a Spanish person is trying to get a job and everything and you're working but now you have to be a lowlife to get help. That's basically what it is according to this younger generation. Only lowlife get on welfare. You can get all these benefits you don't want; they make you lazy. It's discrimination against class. (Cecilia)

Olivia talked of her mother's success at keeping her family happy and clothed despite the grinding poverty of farm work. "You don't live off of nobody. We didn't even know we were poor. I'm not kidding. We had nothing, but we didn't know it. We didn't know mom used to go to second hands and places like that to buy our clothes. We didn't have nothing compared to some. She was good at it, that's all I got to say." Even today Olivia and her husband base their family life on cultural morals, "being there for your kids," rather than giving them material things, even though they have a much more comfortable lifestyle than with what she grew up.

Olivia spoke about how the strong commitment to helping each other, taking care of children, sticking together are "what's taught in the house." Mainstream values of individualism and competition are counter to what is reflected in these testimonies. Sandra described how cooperation and "doing the right thing" is valued in her family.

> I see the Chicano family stick together, and they unite when they have problems. They try to work out their problems, trying to do the best they can to make that family back together again. We're always willing to forgive one another in family situations. I'm very proud of the togetherness of our culture.

This sense of togetherness rather than individualism is reflected in Sandra's comments regarding an Anglo friend and her family's differences.

> My friend's family, they're white, and they're all so separate. They have a real separate way of living; they all go their own ways. She has brothers and sisters who live all over the place. It seems like I hardly see any families that are white that really stay together. We just all want to get together and be around each other.

The community of assistance depicted by these individuals also reflects care beyond the family to include neighbors and friends. Carlos says, "If something goes wrong, it's going to take a cop forever to get there, and that's why a lot of times the neighborhood just watches over each other, watching each other's houses, for an example." Norma describes how she views her neighbors.

> The people they are my neighbors, they're my friends. I know them all. A lot of people move in and out; I'll go meet them. I know everybody. This lady is Spanish, this one's black, this one is Puerto Rican (pointing to houses). When the Spanish lady needs help cleaning her home 'cause she's kinda old, I go help her clean her house. We have to help each other, you know.

In a struggle to reclaim what has been lost, people work together in families and communities as they have done for generations constructing a cultural ethnic consciousness that finds a middle ground between integration and separation.

Otherness

This sense that "we have to help each other" suggests an "Otherness" that people feel as they negotiate the cultural borders. Contrasted to the sense of pride one has in the Mexican American (or Spanish) culture, Olivia illustrated the shame she and her sisters felt being Mexican Americans. "We'd go to school and we didn't want to take burritos to school. We were ashamed of that because we figured all these kids are pulling peanut butter and jelly and we're pulling burritos. That was not good for us. Sometimes we would eat them on the sneak and that's sad." Reflecting now on those days, Olivia expressed a sense of wonderment as to how that happened. All her mother's admonitions that she ought to be proud of her heritage didn't carry as much weight when she felt so different and outside the majority group of children.

Bertha related experiences of discrimination from the parents of one of her Anglo friends when she was a young woman. She recalled her awareness of their uneasiness at her presence in their house. "It was hard for her parents to like, even, what's the right word, get used to me. I would go over to her house and they would look at me like, 'Is she Spanish?'" The contradiction for Bertha was due not so much to parental/adult reactions as it was from her Anglo friend's actions. She was used "as a protection" by these so-called white friends, since other students would not bother them when they were with Bertha. Bertha expressed her confusion by all this in telling me, "Yet I was quiet so I didn't understand their reasoning." Protecting white girls appeared to be the trade-off to gaining their acceptance and friendship at whatever level. Margaret reflected on her fights with white girls. "I used to get into fights with white girls, and I thought it was because she was white and I was Mexican, but now I don't believe that it's like that anymore; it's because of how people treated me." Margaret sees the structures of racism at her school that perpetuated difference and recognizes how such institutional racism manifested in the personal confrontations between herself and white girls as individual acts of disrespect and violation.

Margaret also talked of the social prejudice she felt as a young teen shopping in stores and always being watched. She told of being "stared at like I'm going to steal something when I have the money." While her current experiences of difference are not set within the same parameters as in her youth, they continue nonetheless.

In theorizing this notion of difference, it is easy to see how difference and the "Other" is constituted through acts of power, the power of predominant forces, which seek to assimilate and make things similar, the same. Difference is seen as deviant, even deficient, constructed as binaries of dominant/subordinate, good/bad, superior/inferior that have been used since the days of colonization. As Manuel states:

> In this country people speak very little about our culture
> even though we have been in this land for thousands of years.
> After all this time, we are said to belong to a minority culture.
> We even see enemies among other Latinos, and this is all be-
> cause of ignorance and a lack of information about our cul-
> ture, our plight.

Language of Shame and Pride

Although everyone in the study grew up in households where Spanish was spoken, some reported their parents also spoke English. An overwhelming majority of the men and women (90 percent) identified themselves as bilingual. There were no monolingual Spanish speakers in the study, although the older respondents reported using Spanish as much as, if not more than, English. Maria said, "It depends on who I'm talking to. My family and friends and I speak Spanish. When I go out, I speak English." Three individuals, all women, identified themselves as monolingual English having grown up in Spanish-speaking homes but no longer speaking it. Two were in their 20s, the other was in her 40s. The rest of the people fall within a range of proficiency between "not enough to get me through a Mexican restaurant" to "I understand it all but sometimes have trouble completing full sentences" to "we speak both Spanish and English in the family."

Whether they were fluent, knowing Spanish and using it appeared to have high value. When asked why it is important to speak Spanish, recall Carlos who said, "That's what I was brought up as, that's who I am, that's what I did in the past, that's what I do." The importance of language as identity was echoed by all with several variations on this theme. A range of feelings from pride to shame to conflict were evident in the stories people told. Individuals indicated Spanish is very important to know in order to communicate not only with each other, but with Mexicans who may not know English. According to Sandra, "We should all learn it because that's our heritage, that is my culture." Regina told me of her Spanish-only neighbor who relied on her knowledge of Spanish to help her get around in the community. Regina and others spoke of assisting with translation particularly with Mexicans, "It's a good feeling to help someone." Bertha put it succinctly, "I'm Mexican; I think all Mexicans should learn Spanish."

The sense of shame identified by some people was in reference to regret at not speaking Spanish or giving up their first language. Cristina said, "It is my language, and it's hard when people ask, you're Spanish and you don't speak it?" Some bilingual respondents exhibited a sense of guilt that they had lost some of their Spanish and told of "studying" or learning it again. Judith, a woman in her 40s, recalled that when she learned English in school, she would practice at home, and over time, although she and her parents learned English, she had lost her Spanish. "I learned Spanish when I was growing up, then, when I went to kindergarten, I had to learn English. I stopped talking Spanish after that. My mom, she talked in Spanish and half English. My dad, too. I knew how to speak it real good, and I lost it." As an adult who married a Mexican immigrant years later, she finally regained her Spanish language abilities.

There is an alternative view about the importance of Spanish. Olivia talked about her extended family frequently using English, but that it didn't mean they had lost their culture. They "still have the culture, everything about it. We just don't always use the Spanish." Cecilia talked of her teen years and of not using the Spanish she knew. She recalled that not all Chicanas knew Spanish and her friends never pressured her to speak it. "They knew I didn't speak Spanish so it was no big deal, and my girlfriends never enforced that I use it. There was no need for it." The conflict for Cecilia, however, was her regret at not being able to help others who only spoke Spanish.

The role of language as identity is also exposed in people's histories when they first learned English. Most recalled memories of learning English. For some, it was an inevitable part of their education; for others it held pain and regret.

> At school we weren't allowed to speak Spanish. I had to learn English. If you got caught you would get in trouble–couldn't get recess, had to stand in the corner. I don't know if it was right, but it worked. We learned English. (Eduardo)

> I was punished for speaking Spanish. Whenever I got caught, I had to write lines. I must speak English. I must speak English. (Norma)

In recounting her mother's history, which she was collecting as part of a genealogy project she was putting together, Gloria said, "They grew up speaking nothing but Spanish until they got into school, and then they had no choice but to learn English. So they went to a special class to learn English, and that's when they came home and started speaking English. They stopped speaking [Spanish]." Gloria explained further that her mother regretted giving up her language, and talked about her own efforts to now teach her children Spanish.

Another individual recalled the ridicule she endured when she would try to speak English in the local grocery store. The Anglos would laugh at her efforts. Patricia recounted her experiences in the Colorado schools where she had to speak English, unlike the New Mexico schools where she came from. She had trouble speaking, reading, and writing English. Patricia views her English language abilities as "my handicap." She further attributes her school failure to her inability to communicate with others in either English or Spanish.

Jose told me how language discrimination continues in his life. "It happens at work too. If we speak Spanish, they give us the hard jobs, and the easy jobs go to the ones who can speak English." After recounting his history of learning English at home, since "Mom thought we should get in the flow and learn English; it would be easier for us," and still being ignored in school and not getting the attention he wanted, you will recall Jose's anger. "Anglos say you're dumb if you don't know English. We say we're dumb if we don't know Spanish." Although Jose tells of his pride in being bilingual and his ability to communicate with more people, he also indicated he feels cheated since it never helped him get the jobs he really wanted.

The struggle over language is especially telling and representative of the ongoing conflict. There is a general sense of loss regarding the Spanish language. Forced to assimilate into the dominant culture by accommodating to different cultural values and language, this loss is experienced variably as regret, shame, and conflict. For most, the accommodation has not paid off, and there is a growing movement to relearn or reintegrate Spanish into everyday public life. Not only is Spanish the first language of all participants, but it has become a way of reaffirming a positive sense of self and group identity. Openly using one's language increases pride in who one is. In addition to more public use of the Spanish language, as immigration from Mexico continues to grow, the Mexican American ethos of assistance and care become both more accepted and more integrated into the larger culture. A recent popular magazine article (Tumulty 2001) suggests that this acceptance may be due to the huge growth of Hispanics, now the largest minority group in diverse cities, suburbs, and rural areas across the United States.

Nonetheless, language difference is viewed by the dominant culture as deviance from both cultural and linguistic norms. The ridicule and punishment experienced for "speaking who you are" contributes to an underlying, although increasingly open, sense of outrage and indignation that people feel as they attempt to use their Spanish language as one dimension in cultural-ethnic self-formation.

The importance of regaining one's language was expressed in varying ways people deal with renewed learning of Spanish. Descriptions of having friends teach them Spanish, accounts of losing Spanish language skills while learning English and now using more Spanish again, sending their children to Spanish-speaking preschools and elementary schools, and listening to Spanish music are some of the ways individuals pursue and affirm cultural continuity. If given a choice of assimilation or integration, they prefer to retain their language and cultural identity while at the same time trying to attain economic and social equality. To give up one's language means giving up or compromising who one is without benefit of access to the dominant culture.

Group Ethos

A group ethos, or group identity, exists as evidenced in the individual accounts of ancestry and nativity as well as from accounts of the lived experiences of community, language, and struggle. This group ethos is informed by a shared past of belonging to an indigenous people of the Mexico, New Mexico, and Colorado corridor in which families did whatever it took to maintain community and familial ties, economic independence, and cultural autonomy in the face of colonization. Jose's words speak of this wisdom. "We talked about how Latinos are often put down as if they belonged in a lower level. I am convinced we can do something about it and struggle [against it]. If we only do what others say, we have no life of our own, and in the process, the little we know of ourselves will be destroyed."

Kinship networks, strategies for economic survival, and regional communities stressed staying connected not only to each other but to their heritage as well. This shared past creates a collective memory. Similar patterns of coping, which influence and promote meaning in everyday life, are still utilized as seen in the stories of individual and group assistance and care, and a sense of togetherness. These are traditions of cultural and ethnic survival.

Included in these documented stories is evidence of relying on one's family, and the group as a whole, to help meet the challenges and struggles of existence rather than turning to outside assistance. There is also evidence of reciprocal group support for those who are in need, thus indicating an ethic of care. This ethic of care is characterized by a "family atmosphere" and shared responsibility. Out of this cultural ethic, a community of assistance is formed whereby group advancement, as well as individual advancement, is valued. In order for this advancement to occur, people cooperate with each other and collaborate with each other to meet common needs.

The group ethos is also formed and transformed by interactions with the dominant culture. Experiences of exclusion, struggles, and inequalities in social, economic, and political situations conflict with their everyday practices of care and assistance. While individual experiences differ, contemporary subjectivities suggest multiple and variegated tensions and contradictions. Reflecting on everyday life experiences of labor and work abuse, community neglect by government agencies, lack of police protection, prejudice and discrimination experienced at personal and group levels, indicates people's awareness of their role and value, or lack thereof, within the larger community.

For the most part, individuals and their families have attempted to acculturate into the dominant society while retaining and maintaining their cultural identity. Olivia's assessment that "we were always the outsiders" captures the contradictions of striving for equality without success. The struggle over language portrays the dialectical interplay between social structures and human agency. As people have tried to fit into the mainstream, they are continually rejected. Yet as they resist the dominant discourse that defines them as outsiders, they continue to press up against discrimination and unequal institutions that attempt to assimilate them into the dominant culture.

Mexican Americans live in two worlds. As subordinated people, continually moving back and forth across cultural borders, they interface with the contemporary power structure of mainstream society and its dominant values of Eurocentric individualism, competition, and middle-class privilege. The multicultural and multivaried experiences of individuals socially constructed around race, ethnicity, class, and gender influence and create a politics of identity and group ethos dependent upon everyday practices and discourses. Identity politics and the group ethos, however, are not unidirectional. In other words, identity and group ethos are not only influenced and created by socially constructed experiences, but also influence and create everyday decision making as it relates to social interactions. One's identity with a group formed out of a shared past, reinforced by lived traditions and values, and influenced by interactions with other diverse groups, impacts moral and ethical decision making in everyday life. The whole of one's subjectivity constrained by social structures and embedded in contemporary ideological, economic, and political practices influences perspectives and subsequent modes of action.

Chapter 4
The Double Bind of Youth:
Desire, Schooling, and Power

Amidst the hegemony of schooling, voices of struggle and re-sistance can be seen to emerge. (Walsh 1991, 59)

The dominant discourse promotes education as the required creden-tial that will provide access to economic and social mobility and will en-able people to participate fully in the social, civic, political, and eco-nomic aspects of society. Yet, historical contexts of education, learning, and literacy are factors that influence individual decisions and actions in furthering one's efforts to meet educational needs and desires.

Focusing the lens more narrowly, we turn to people's experiences in various school settings in New Mexico and Colorado as youth who were, at one time, filled with hope. I was interested in how people viewed their early years of education and the key events that were em-bedded in their memories. What were their experiences as a minority group member, and how did they perceive those experiences? What factors and stories held the most power? Through a series of questions about the learning environment, teacher and peer interactions, academic success and struggles, ethnicity, culture and identity, I hoped to get a glimpse into their educational histories. As people reflected on those days, I heard stories that were powerful reminders of difference, discrimination, and struggle.

The types of schools they attended included integrated, Anglo, and segregated schools. Integrated schools were of two subtypes; in some, the majority of students were Anglo but included African Americans and Latinos/as, while in other integrated schools, Latinos/as and African American students were the majority with a small number of Anglos. These differences depended on whether the school was located in a predominately white neighborhood or a predominately minority one. Segregated schools also were of two subtypes; individuals described schools that enrolled only students of color, while others described Anglo schools where only a small handful of individuals of color were enrolled.

All of the men and women have been out of school quite a long time, except for a couple young women who were nineteen years old when I talked with them. Still, the stories they tell about their school days are fresh memories, as if they have been told and retold or held in a special space for reflection and healing. Very often, studies of high school noncompleters hoist the blame of underachievement and noncompletion onto the individual student without considering the structural and cultural constraints these youth must contend with as they pursue educational requirements and interests.

Youth Education

All individuals left school prior to completing requirements for a high school diploma or, in some cases, prior to achieving basic English literacy skills of reading and writing. The majority of individuals left during their eleventh year of schooling. Some had tried alternative schools between their tenth and eleventh year, but found alternatives in bad areas of town or where gangs ruled the school. They also told of alternative schools that had stricter attendance requirements and tighter rules of discipline.

Alternative schools grew out of the new sociology of schooling during the 1960s as an alternative to the public school system, which was under scrutiny by liberals and progressives who claimed schooling was not responsive to the youth who did not fit into the dominant culture. Such educators as Jonathan Holt, Ivan Illich, and others critiqued traditional K-12 education by developing models that were learner-centered and used strategies such as open classrooms, student-identified curriculum, and alternative assessments. Alternative schools initially existed outside the traditional schooling system and found varying success. Alternative ideologies and methodologies were developed and some schools, like Summerhill, were very successful. In other areas of the country, community schools were an outgrowth of this movement with heavy parental involvement in management and curriculum being a hallmark of the new schools. Over time public school districts became interested in the concept of alternative schools. Public alternative high schools adapted some of the ideas of open schools, or free schools as they were often called, to fit the limits of public schooling. The magnet school grew out of this alternative education movement and provided additional models of classroom organization and curriculum delivery.

I was part of this alternative school movement in a large midwestern school district by coauthoring a proposal to the district outlining a model that could be incorporated into the traditional structure. The school district was interested because of the high dropout rate and the perceived social problems of the schools in minority and low-income neighborhoods. The district saw our model, which grew out of our experiences working in several independent alternative schools, as a hopeful solution for the youth who had become disenfranchised with the traditional system. Unfortunately, one of the backlashes of public alternative schools is that youth are directed by counselors to these schools once they have been labeled troublemakers or have attendance problems. This is similar to what we found in the independent alternatives. In other words, the public alternative schools, similar to the independents, became dumping grounds for youth who are considered to be disruptive to traditional school life.

The students' disillusionment with public education often grew out of rebellion to conformity and imposed external controls, inappropriate tracking into lower-skill courses or courses that were not self-chosen, ineffectual teachers who could not teach beyond the white, middle-class norm, and incompatible ideology of individualized competition; a school system organized around patriarchy and racism. Individualized problems masked the social structural inadequacies that exist within public education.

While some public alternative high schools are a viable way to complete school for many students, for others, these alternatives have similar problems to the schools they left that make them just as unattractive as the traditional high schools. Over time, some alternative high schools have become corrupt providing low quality education or disorganized learning. Additionally, due to the location of many alternative high schools in low-income neighborhoods, they are seen as undesirable and not offering anything more for disenfranchised youth than the traditional models.

Elena reported signing up for the alternative school, however, she said she never attended as a result of years of frustration as "being a loner and not fitting in."

> I was very shy all through school, so much of a loner. I wasn't going to class so why finish. My sister talked me into trying the alternative school so I went once to enroll but decided not to go back because I didn't know anyone.

For Linda, a teen mother, the alternative high school did not provide her with the solution to finishing her education.

> I was fifteen years old and had a child. I went to the alternative school where they worked with you a lot, but it was too hard with a child. At my other high school, the teachers didn't like you; they didn't help you.

Alternative high schools with nontraditional approaches to education and smaller class sizes often provide teen mothers the type of one-on-one support they need in order to get through school, but for Linda, the demands of being a parent at such an early age coupled with the continuing demands of schooling were just too much for her. Likewise, for Gloria, the assistance she needed in catching up on credits was not available at the alternative program she attended.

> I went to the alternative school in eleventh grade to catch up on credits. If they had done that, I'd probably have my GED, if I would have had a counselor to help me.

Gloria, like others, expected the alternative school counselor to direct her and help her reach her goals of high school completion. Sandra experienced another alternative school as cumbersome, tangled in "red tape," and even though she wanted to go back, she attributes her decision to stay out of school as determined by "more important" things such as peer pressure and lifestyle rather than the institutional problems she identified. There is a consistent tendency for individuals to fault themselves for not completing their education. Listen to Sandra.

> I was going to start going over there to that alternative school after I dropped out of high school. I was nineteen years old. I went and got enrolled and everything and never went back. They told me the paperwork that I needed. I went in there and gave them the little bit of paperwork that I had, and they said they needed more paperwork and other stuff. You needed stuff from way back, at the time I was living alone. A lot of red tape, and so I never went back.

> When I decided to go back to school after dropping out, I decided I have to make it right because I have to get a good job, something that I'm going to be able to do with my life since I'm out on my own. I just wanted to go to school for that, and then every time something else would come up where I thought it was more important to me than school.

> That's because of me though; I chose not to go back because I was into the party scene so bad, and I just thought that's all I wanted to do with my life.

The decision "to make it right" contradicted Sandra's choice "not to go back." How large of a role did the school's need for "more paper work and other stuff" play in her decision to walk away?

Another strategy people used to side-step educational obstacles was to enroll in other schools within the same school district or leave their official home district entirely. Moving from one school to another, Carlos recalled trying two other high schools before reaching the age of twenty-one in order to get the required credits for graduation. Several women told of attending high schools outside their districts. Sylvia, for example, related her strategy of moving in with an aunt who lived in a suburban area in order to "concentrate on studying." The school office found out she had lied about her permanent address, since she would go to her neighborhood home on weekends. As a result, she was asked to leave the suburban school.

Several individuals left during or right after junior high school, never reaching high school. Most of them talked about dramatic differences between elementary school and junior high. They spoke of how elementary school was "fun," they had "nice teachers," they got "good grades," "I loved science," "I was great at spelling;" whereas junior high was characterized by images of "things changed," "trouble," "turmoil," "punishment," and "discourage[ment]."

The differences between elementary and junior and senior high school are well documented in research literature and present pressing dilemmas for educators. The transition from self-contained classrooms to more freedom and movement from one class to another are often cited as two organizational shifts that cause many youth problems and disorientation to schooling. Nevertheless, viewed as a socializing structure, schooling strategies used in the junior and high school environments seek to exert more control over students, not less, as is portrayed. As children become more mature and can make more sophisticated decisions and choices, they find themselves in systems that strive to "monoculture" (Vogel Zanger 1994) students to fit in and conform to the dominant culture standard. It is no wonder that individuals report dramatic changes from elementary settings into junior and high school environments.

For Ana, grade school held the fondest memories, but when she got to high school, she found teachers who were not as caring as her favorite elementary teacher.

> [The elementary teacher] go, whenever you need help on your math, let me know, and we'll just do it right here. I can help you. That's how I got real good at my math 'cause she'd really helped me constantly in the classroom. I didn't expect her just to help me, she needs to help everybody. She said if I had trouble to just come in after school. She helped me a lot.
>
> Elementary school was fun, but things were different in high school. Teachers were not into it; they were just there. They didn't care.

Caring then becomes the initial benchmark for judging one educational environment from the other, rather than an awareness of, or perhaps acknowledgment of, structural changes. Ana felt her shyness was the reason she did not learn to read, hoisting the blame for not liking school or doing well onto herself.

I've been shy around the classroom. I think that's why I lost a
lot on my reading cause I'd be shy to ask for help and all that.
I would be shy that's why I'd tell myself, don't be shy—you
need help, you ask them teachers, that's what they're there
for, to teach.

The desire to fit in was strong for Sandra, and it colored her junior
and high school decisions. Involvement with her peer group was very
important to her sense of belonging, and she chose that over academic
involvement. Belonging, as a basic survival need, is something people
must have in order gain a sense of security, and security is often a pre-
requisite if learning is going to occur. Sandra also told me of using in-
timidation and fighting with the white girls who were the cheerleaders
believing they thought they were better than her. Her peer-group identification was thus reinforced.

Maybe it was my own insecurity. I always had it in my mind,
that they thought they were better than me. I would fight
with them. They wouldn't fight back with me because they
were too afraid of me. I hate to say it, but I was just a fighter.
When you are young you don't think about consequences
you have to face when you're doing those kinds of things.

I was into a lot of just being with friends and hanging out and
drinking and doing all the things I wasn't supposed to be doing, getting involved with the wrong crowd and not going to
class, that was basically it. I was good in school, but I just
thought my friends were more important than school was at
the time. If people choose the wrong way to go, if they start
hanging out with people that are an influence that's a problem. Some people are followers, and some are leaders. I happened to be a follower, followed the crowd, I wanted to be
part of the crowd. I didn't have any interest in school at all.

The rest of the people left school during their sophomore year of
high school. These individuals related dramatic changes between junior high and senior high. For some it was grades, for some it was the
teachers' attitudes, for all, it was a different environment from what
they had previously experienced. Individuals spoke of teacher insensitivity, unsafe learning conditions, frustration with courses that weren't
challenging, and a lack of trust between teachers and students.

Cultural roles of Mexican Americans also figured into reasons for
leaving school as well as family poverty where one was needed to help
with financial obligations. Cecilia related to me the importance her

parents placed on completing school so that their children would not have the hard life they were living, but embedded in Cecilia's comments are traces of cultural norms and expectations of male and female roles that guided her thinking and decision making.

> To look back, they really impressed on us to go to school, "look at us; we have to work so hard." Well, if you're a man, of course, you're going to work hard. Being raised with so many boys, I was a tomboy all the way. I didn't think I needed all that stuff [education]. I was going to end up like my sisters-in-law; my brothers did not let them go to work at that time. Yeah, a man was a man, a woman was a woman, you stay home and do this and do that. With the older brothers, you see their wives working but not too much. I didn't ever picture myself in that situation. I thought I'll get married, and that's basically what I thought.

Olivia also mentioned the role her parents played in her education. While she told me she made sure she went to all her children's school activities to show support, her mother was not able to do that because of the young children still at home. Further, Olivia indicated her mother's traditional expectations for her daughter's life were an important factor in leaving school.

> When I was growing up, when I was being educated, going to school, parents back then, the majority of them sent their children to school only because it was the law. You had to go to school to a certain age, and that was all there was to it. If you got good grades fine, if you didn't, your parents kind of sensed how you [would do]. All you're going to do is get married and have kids, and you don't get encouraged differently. I quit in the ninth grade, and there was nothing to it. Like I said, parents back then, I'm not saying all, I can't judge for all, but the majority of parents back then said, quit and stay home and learn how to be a woman and be a mother and cook, and that's exactly what I did. My mother had me help her with the girls because she had a lot of children.

Family expectations coupled with poverty were potent reasons for leaving school, but when students are bored because teachers are not responsive, it gives them no reason to stay. Ana related her situation in which she could not relate to any of the other students once her friends left. Often skipping school, Ana claimed she was bored without her friends. Teachers called her mother alerting her of the absences.

Eventually, Ana's mother encouraged her to make a decision to attend classes if she was going to stay in school or officially drop out. Ana chose to leave.

> I come from a big family and my mom couldn't afford to buy us clothes and that. So I said I'll just make my own money and buy my own clothes. I needed some money to buy clothes and all; it was hard on my mom. None of us graduated, not even one out of 15. A lot of them got their GED, my sister and a few of my brothers. There are a few of my brothers, they can't read at all. I don't know why, I think my mother sent them to school. I know she did.

> I think I was bored [in school]. I mean my classes were fun, but my friends weren't going there no more. It was boring. So it was mostly myself because I was taking some fun classes. I got bored by myself. The teachers were friendly, real nice. I had good teachers, no complaints. They were fair. My mom would get mad; she'd say, I'm getting tired of these teachers calling you. She said if you don't want to go to school then quit so I kept going 'til I was seventeen then I quit. I just dropped out.

While the reasons people left school varied, there are patterns to their experiences while in school. Teacher insensitivity, safety issues, lack of counseling assistance, differential discipline, and cultural differences were themes that emerged from the collective stories. Descriptions of these concepts create images of lack of care on the part of teachers and administrators, a breakdown of trust between teacher and student, measures and mechanisms used for control, and lack of quality in educational programs and settings. A broader lens was used to refocus these themes into core properties that include teacher attitudes, academic discrimination, and cultural respect.

Teacher Attitudes

The attitudes of teachers play an important role in the academic success of students. Perceptions regarding the attitudes of teachers were described in terms of neglect, put downs, and inattention.

Bertha recalled that teachers offered no encouragement nor seemed to care if students made the right choices. She holds teachers responsible for not providing guidance and the reason children are leaving school at earlier and earlier ages.

> The teachers didn't give any encouragement; they weren't into it, they were just there. They didn't care if you finished your work or not. The teachers never showed me what's ahead, I think they should have done that. They didn't seem to care what happened to me. Kids need attention. Now it's even worse, kids leaving earlier.

> Teachers pick their favorites, that's where they put their attention. If the kid is not so good, they don't really care even though that person wants to learn.

This lack of care to the extent of "not show[ing] me what's ahead" and further admonitions about "kids need attention" are reflections about how things should have been as compared to how things were. As the mother of two preteens, Bertha expressed concern about what might lie ahead for them. "One is getting ready to go to junior high school and I don't hear good things about it. Do you know anything about it?" Lack of appropriate attention is also apparent in these comments. Cristina explained:

> At the high school, they wouldn't work with us, instead they try to say, "Well, you know, this [white] person is really trying so we'll work with them." I mean how could we really try if they never worked with us, so you know that's another thing.

For Tony, it was a matter of not getting enough attention from the teachers. He was aware of the prejudice that some white teachers had for Chicano/a students, and he attributed the neglect he felt to these attitudes.

> I didn't feel I was getting as much attention as others. All the teachers were Anglos. They had this attitude thing. They didn't care if I was there; they didn't notice whether or not I was there. I can't push it all on prejudice, but it was there. It didn't matter to teachers, they'd say, figure it out yourself. Can't blame me 'cause teachers didn't care to help, but there was no reason to stay.

Regina, on the other hand, experienced this lack of care as indifference on the part of the teachers where she was expected to figure things out for herself. Underlying her description of remembered experiences is the assumption that if teachers cared, they would provide the assistance students need.

> Here's a paper, do it and turn it in, nothing else; and you'd go to them for help, and they would just write it on the board. They wouldn't tell you how to figure it out, nothing, they'd just write it on the board; you figure it out yourself. I don't know that it mattered to any of them.

Both Tony and Regina have expectations that teachers are there to help them understand the content of the curriculum, and when this does not occur, it is the fault of the teachers who seem indifferent or discriminate in terms of who they will spend their time helping. Awareness of the differences in attention, whether due to racial differences, differences of effort, or lack of interest, have not been forgotten as the participants' statements indicate. The attention individuals sought was not personal attention but rather academic guidance, learning assistance, and teaching instruction, reasonable requests in an educational setting. The social dynamics of schooling experienced by these individuals resulted in alienation, silencing, and a decline in motivation.

There was a lack of trust between teachers and students. Trust as it relates to "knowing" and "legitimate knowledge" appeared to be in question. Relating experiences of gang violence in her school, Julia told of her efforts to avoid involvement with the women of a female African American gang. She related an incident where gang members threatened her and detained her from getting to class on time. When she told the teacher, the teacher wouldn't believe her. Julia said it was a common occurrence, and she had reported it to the principal's office several times. The young woman's comments about the teachers included:

> My family needed the income, making the bills, so I left school when I was seventeen. I was having trouble with gangs bothering me. I would report it to the office but no one would do anything or believe me. The NS mafia girls threatened me but didn't do anything to me. I couldn't get to classes because they stopped me. The teachers were not easy to talk to. They already know the students they want in school. They didn't accept me, I had too many attendance problems. They wanted to send me to the alternative school but I didn't want to go, there was just as much trouble there.

Reading the subtext, Julia is telling us that she was not one of those students who fit in, and teachers attitudes towards her eroded her trust both of the teachers and the school environment. Her safety needs were not taken seriously, nor did teachers seem to care that she might be having problems with gang members. When initially asked why she had left school, Julia told me it was because her family needed financial assistance so she left to get a job and help out. Only later did she reveal the real reason she left, fear for her safety. Whether out of fear or neglect, the teachers in this situation, as agents of the state, allowed Julia to take the only recourse left to her, that of leaving school. Favoritism towards those students who fit or conform to the standards over those who some teachers might find difficult to understand is evident here.

Jimmy reported similar experiences with gang harassment and he requested a transfer to the alternative school. His request was denied by the principal who told him, "You're not going to get anywhere if you won't face your problems." For whatever reason, Jimmy's assessment of the situation he found himself in did not carry any weight with the principal, thus breaking any degree of trust that Jimmy might have had in getting the support for which he was looking. Finally, this statement from Roberto signified the essence of hopelessness and closed options within the educational system.

> I wanted to transfer out because of the violence in the school but they didn't want to transfer me to any place else. You know, if you're in this district you can't go any place else. So there wasn't really much of a chance for me anyway.

Bertha got involved with a girl gang at the predominately Chicano/a school she attended. She took the basic courses open to her, such as home economics and woodshop, but was not good in math. Regretting those days, Bertha said, "There wasn't really a chance for me anyway." She didn't get any encouragement from the teachers, whom she felt should have guided her and told her what was ahead.

Put-downs from teachers were another set of actions described. Put-downs are verbal acts of violence. Put-downs erode trust and indicate a type of contempt that some have carried for a long time.

> I had this one teacher cuss me out, an English teacher, so I stopped going to her class, but I would go to my other classes. Then the principal told me he didn't want me back. The teachers would just tell you, like, you ain't going to make it in life if you keep doing this and doing that. They weren't

helping, they were always putting you down, they always put someone down, they would take it out on a lot of students.

The aforementioned statement was made by Judith who tried going to high school as a young mother. She had to go home at lunch time to switch babysitters, and she would be up late at night finishing her homework. She continued in this situation for a full school year but was unable to sustain the struggle and persevere in a situation that provided no support for her.

Academic Discrimination

When asked about their academic experiences, people identified several types of discrimination. Comments were classified into four sub-categories including academic ability, tracking, quality of classes, and counseling. Academic ability appeared to be secondary in relation to class assignment as presented by Elena. Relating a series of experiences in a prealgebra course she commented:

> I was put in this lower class. I had asked for an algebra course, which I could do, but was put in prealgebra instead. I'd go ahead of the book, and the teacher would tell me not to do that, "When I say to go on, then go on, but not before." I went to class for the final and got a good grade, but I didn't go every day. Instead of judging me by what I could do, they were judging me according to attendance.

Elena was subtly told through this experience not to aim too high. She also told of teachers who would stay on the same subject for three and four weeks at a time. She was frustrated by the slow pace—"show something and go on" was her attitude. Elena judged herself as being held back and not allowed to excel. Having little recourse, she learned on her own by jumping ahead and tackling the lessons further on in the math book.

Discrimination through academic tracking was described by Gloria as she related her husband's experiences in high school.

> My husband, when he was going to school, at the time, the teachers told him—well he says, I'll take this class and this class, and they said, you'll never become more than a labor worker, you don't need that. They set that in his mind that he would never accomplish to really succeed in life.

Goals and desires on the part of individuals are not taken into account, rather a preset view of where a person belongs is often used in scheduling classes. "You'll never become more than a labor worker, you don't need that" is blatantly discriminatory, and Gloria was not going to let it go unnoticed. There are underlying and lasting contradictions in the structural mechanisms employed in educational institutions that suggest that while individuals can participate in schooling, they cannot direct the outcome no matter what their effort. Patricia was similarly aware that she was put in lower classes. Settling for what she could get she was, nevertheless, disappointed that she was not smart like the whites students she observed. She attributed her status to language difference, a personal deficit, but the tracking achieved the same dampening effect that is evident in Elena's and Gloria's comments above.

> I knew I was in a lower class all through high school and it was because of my language. I didn't understand it all though. I would see what the whites were doing, and I always wanted to be like them—smart. I finally settled for what I could do.

Carlos and Roberto talked about how they were scheduled for extra or double gym classes; Sandra's ideas of basic courses were the home economic and woodshop courses she took; and Regina indicated she took courses every semester in things like child care, home economics, and business-related skills such as typing, filing, and office work. In none of the accounts did people tell about being on an academic or college track, although as Elena pointed out, she had the ability and desire to do algebra rather than the lower-track math she was assigned.

Academic discrimination goes beyond course scheduling. The quality of instruction, differences in course offerings and content, and school equipment are more likely determined by where one lives than what students need or want. Describing the differences between the education her children were getting living in an integrated neighborhood (a conscious choice to avoid the differentials of Denver's inner-city schools) and the education a friend's children living in the inner-city were receiving, Olivia stated:

> So they're in the same grade, all these kids, and she was showing me what they were being taught, and I was saying what my kids were being taught, and let me tell you, there was a big, big difference, a very big difference. And I'm

thinking, what in the world. She goes, "I wish my kids could go to school where yours are going." That bothered me, I felt bad for them especially knowing that they were Chicano kids. I thought that's not cool, that's not fair.

Recall that Olivia also related differences in school offerings based on her own experiences as she was growing up in Greeley. There was an Anglo school and a Chicano/a school. Starting out at the Chicano/a school, Olivia moved to the Anglo school when her family moved from one of the Chicano/a colonias into the city.

> It makes a difference; it makes a difference what they offer you in a white school than what you get offered somewhere else.

Finally, counseling, as a mechanism for assisting individuals in the choice of courses and career direction, was seen as a service that was withheld. The differentials in counseling services were seen to impact both academic direction and eventual economic success. Patricia told me:

> I never saw my counselor in high school because they were probably saying, Oh she's not college material—which I really wasn't. I wasn't even school material. (Patricia)

> I mean everybody had a counselor back then in high school; but they didn't really take a personal interest in you. They didn't really push you, you know. (Gloria)

Gloria's similar experience suggests that both women expected counselors to take an active interest and role in their education guiding them along with advice and support when that was what was needed rather than seeing the counselor as the person who guides one in the selection of courses. Academic differentials, whether viewed as lack of counseling and career advice, tracking into lower-level courses or into a direction different from the one desired, ignoring academic ability by focusing on school rules and regulations, or limiting the access to quality educational choices, have created memories deeply embedded in these personal histories affecting perceptions of schooling for their own children and other Chicanos/as.

Cultural Regard

The final category depicting educational experiences of youth is cultural regard. Testimony represents notions of racial disrespect, prejudice, economic elitism, and subordination. Olivia put it succinctly.

> We were always the outsiders. I remember this one [white] kid that just because he was poor, these whites, they totally just made a mess of his life. At least us, we could say, oh well, I guess it's just because the color of our skin. Because they're poor, you're prejudiced? They wouldn't even want to get near him.

Sandra related her experience of showing her Chicana pride, which was not shared by the Anglo administrators at the school she attended.

> I can remember one time I was wearing this shirt. We used to wear shirts that had green sleeves and then one white and one red panel with the Chicano colors, and it said "Thank God I'm Chicano." It was a fad, you know. The assistant principal told me I shouldn't be wearing those kind of things to school. You know, I had the right to wear whatever I pleased. I'm proud of who I am. He didn't have no business telling me that.

As was discussed previously, cultural identity is closely tied to language. According to Carlos, "If you lose your language, you lose everything." The following comments indicate a common experience of individuals who were Spanish-speaking as youth. Spanish was not tolerated in the schools during the 1960s and 1970s when these individuals attended.

> I went to school in New Mexico. The teacher made fun of me, in front of the whole class, for speaking Spanish. (Norma)

> At school we weren't allowed to speak Spanish. I had to learn English. My teachers would say, "Speak English, this is America, or you'll have to sit in the corner." (Eduardo)

> I didn't know English. That's why I couldn't spell because I didn't know what I was reading or writing. Well, it was only here in Colorado Springs. Back home (New Mexico) it wasn't like that, you know. It was, as a matter of fact, there

wasn't even a white teacher. They were all Mexican, Spanish-speaking teachers. (Patricia)

We spoke nothing but Spanish at home until we got into school. We had no choice but to learn English. I had a hard time because my parents spoke Spanish and I had to switch all the time from Spanish to English to Spanish. (Manuel)

In these accounts, we hear the pain of speaking one's native language as well as the individual and family struggles of adjusting to a new language. Patricia took the judgement onto her own shoulders calling her language a handicap, which held her back academically throughout her educational career. Eduardo assesses the effect of being punished for speaking Spanish as not right. He went on to say, "It's sad to say, most of the time, we're followers. We're not leaders in this United States of ours." Learning English out of fear of being punished silences both the English voice and the Spanish voice of individuals. Not being allowed to speak the language, which is comfortable yet considered by teachers as inappropriate in an English-speaking classroom, nonetheless, challenges one's self-esteem. These practices attempt to strip not only language but culture and identity. There must be another way to encourage development of English language skills than having to give up who you are.

Jose reported that he and his brothers were the only Mexicans in the school they attended. As a result of his mother's attitude about English, "Mom thought we should get in the flow and learn English, it would be easier for us," Jose and his brothers spoke English. "At one time, a Chicano had an advantage over an Anglo if he was bilingual, but what happened is Anglos are taking Spanish classes and taking jobs again."

Nevertheless, Jose recalled being ignored and not noticed by teachers. His assessment of the situation determined it was based on his race. An individual's defense of his culture does not mean that he does not want to succeed in the dominant culture. Rather, Chicanos/as seek an additive rather than a subtractive educational context where their language and culture is not replaced with another.

The Double Bind

Within the categories of teacher attitude, academic discrimination, and cultural respect, the attributes in each case indicate differential treatment. This differential treatment, as related to teacher attitudes, included qualities of lack of care, breakdown of trust, put-downs, and lack of teaching and learning assistance. Within the category of academic discrimination, the differential attributes include education tracking, lack of counseling assistance, and lack of academic quality and options. Finally, looking at cultural respect, individuals in this study described differential discipline based on race and ethnicity and punishment for using their primary language.

Teacher attitudes that are nonsupportive and, in fact, include discriminatory practices, ridicule and put-downs, combined with academic experiences that have tracked individuals into programs they do not want or into situations without benefit of counseling assistance, along with a lack of cultural respect for diversity of culture and language, create negative memories of the junior high and high school years for these individuals. This is not to say that all individuals experienced all situations, but rather to illustrate the linkages that exist to produce a generalized view of differentials and negative experiences. In whatever combination, individuals experienced differential treatment during those educational years. The response, nevertheless, was the same; these individuals left school.

Chronologically speaking, schooling is one of the first prominent social institutions that an individual experiences along with family, religion, and community. Although individuals related little about initial schooling experiences, there were notations made of difficult transitions between elementary and junior high schooling. For some, there were equally difficult transitions when they entered high school. Individuals voiced differences in reference to academics as well as relations with teachers and peers.

The role of education, as a socializing mechanism for the integration of individuals into the dominant culture, is exemplified in the texts of people's lives. As individuals prepare themselves to enter the mainstream and take their place as contributing adult members, schooling prepares them for their roles. Based on expectations, needs, and desires, informed by a group ethos of shared ethnic values in the later years of their youth, individuals look to the schools they attend, the teachers and administrators they encounter there, and their peers to assist them in their transition into the economic, political, ideological, and social realms of the dominant society. However, education, espousing the official view of society, foreshadows the partially-closed society that they are to enter; a society that denies equal and equitable access. In other words, the educational system prepares individuals, through academic discrimination and exclusion, attitudes of inattention and neglect, and cultural difference and elitism, to take their subordinated place in society. Schools are sites of symbolic violence, which mirror larger social systems.

In response to the conflict between these everyday experiences and their cultural values, individuals rejected their subordinate status by leaving environments that reflected that status. However, a further conflict complicates individual decisions to leave school. These individuals want an education and perceive themselves to have needs and desires that have not been satisfied. The educational ideology espoused by the dominant culture promotes education as the requirement for economic access and social mobility. These individuals wanted that access and that mobility. This puts people in a double bind. As youth, they chose to reject the particular settings they were in by walking away, yet they yearned for the opportunity to participate in and contribute to mainstream life. In either case, their testimony documents the difficulty they have had in getting an education that meets their standards of equity and quality.

Some teachers and policy makers describe these individuals as "dropouts." It may be more appropriate to call them "jumpouts" based on their efforts to secure a safe environment for themselves to learn while attempting to obtain English literacy skills and a high school credential. They also may appropriately be viewed as "pushouts" based on education's role of socializing individuals for subordinate status and the hostility directed towards them because of their cultural differences. Since these students were not willing to assimilate into the system, they were pushed to the margins.

Racial prejudice, as the means to their subordinate status as described by these individuals, documents the historical contexts of their past educational experiences. The meaning learners make is informed by these social conditions that promote subsequent actions to fight oppression. Walking away from situations that are not life affirming suggests individuals have monitored both the social interactions of the situations and their own conduct. If the past informs the present, what understandings and resources have people gained that they can use in contemporary decision making? As adults, their perceptions and the decisions they make regarding further actions to meet their educational needs are influenced by these past experiences as well as by their own responses to the discriminatory practices.

Chapter 5
Repeat Performance:
Pedagogy in Adult Education

> Consider this: if someone knows something but cannot gain the agreement of anyone else at all, the product of that knowing has not been called knowledge and may well be suspected to be the product of madness—even if perhaps inspired madness. Similarly, if a nonlegitimate group knows something and makes claims for its general validity, what is known is easily written off as prejudice, merely experiential, biased or ignorant by the legitimate authorities. (Minnich 1990, 151)

Literacy practitioners and policy makers often believe that those individuals who are not engaged in formalized adult programs have a low perception of their educational needs. Such assumptions regarding people's interest in adult education programs may be erroneous. A majority of individuals indicated efforts to return to school to upgrade academic and vocational skills, thus suggesting that there may be reasons why people do not enroll and participate in adult basic education and

English literacy programs other than not recognizing their own educational needs.

Here we examine the types of adult education programs that some people have attended at various points in their adult lives followed by their perceptions of their experiences with those programs. A comparison of the similarities between their educational experiences as youth and as adults is discussed.

Although I was interviewing people who were not enrolled in adult basic education and English literacy programs, talking with Maria alerted me to the possibility that people might have participated in adult basic education or English literacy activities at some time in their pasts. As profiled in Maria's account, she had little formal education due to her family responsibilities for her siblings. Yet I learned she had engaged in several attempts to learn to read English through church-based tutoring programs. Although short-lived, Maria's use of tutors to help her improve her English certainly indicated continued efforts to improve skills.

When I questioned the other men and women, I found that the majority of them also had in the past participated, sometimes repeatedly, to upgrade or improve academic and vocational skills by attending either adult basic education and English literacy or high school completion programs. All indicated a lack of educational or academic fulfillment and a desire for more learning opportunities. Since it was not the intent of this study to test and place people's academic skills of reading and writing, no attempt at assessment was conducted. Most individuals, however, indicated they believed they had low-level reading and writing skills or were not able to read at all, had problems pronouncing certain words, could not remember math, had limited reading comprehension or poor spelling abilities. This information was always volunteered. The point here is simply that people perceived themselves to have educational needs and desires that have not been satisfied.

Efforts to Return to School

A large number of those who reported past efforts to return to school said they had made several attempts. While these repeated efforts might indicate people are looking for an appropriate fit between their desires and what programs offer, their comments and stories would indicate that there is more than just a question of a "comfortable fit."

As I listened to individual accounts of concrete educational situations, the details of lived experiences, several themes emerged from the statements including intercultural understanding, teacher attitudes, pedagogy, curriculum, teaching-learning exchange, and peers. Refocusing these into a broader lens, three final themes were identified: marginalization, learning expectations, and intercultural understanding. The textual language was then analyzed for imagery relating to Chicano/a positions within the learning environment. This discourse analysis yielded additional themes of invisibility, lack of care, struggle, difference, subordination, and exclusion.

Marginalization

Based on adult education experiences, individuals described what it feels like to exist on the social and academic margins in learning settings. People recounted stories of being left to fend for themselves in understanding course material, maneuvering racial boundaries, and having difficulties in working with instructors. Dimensions of marginalization were characterized by subthemes of exclusion, invisibility, and inferior status. Feelings of exclusion were expressed in relation to other students and to teachers, and invisibility related to a lack of care and attention on the part of the teacher. A sense of inferior status was conveyed by comments and attitudes about the learning environment.

Relationships with instructors and peers take on major importance where interaction is the key to learning. The atmosphere within the classroom has the power to either restrict or encourage the learning process. Some individuals painted pictures of exclusion and voiced this sense with such phrases as "pushed away," "didn't care," "walked away," and "figure it out," that characterized teacher behaviors. Sandra talked about a reading and writing program she had attended several years before and described frustration in not making any headway due to having to figure it out herself because she was getting no help from teachers.

> I wasn't getting any help. I didn't understand what I was
> studying, but I more or less, kind of, had to do it on my own,
> just study up on what I thought was best.

Her sense of being left on her own heightened her isolation from
the help she wanted and needed in order to learn; the subtext of her
statement reflected feelings of neglect and lack of care. A sense of
wanting to be a part of the learning group was expressed by Ana who
questioned the teaching strategy of the individualized instruction she
encountered in an adult lab program. Separated from both teacher and
peers, isolated learning is the unintended outcome of self-paced individualized learning situations. Ana said,

> It was hard, they just give you a book and say—here do it. I
> liked sometimes for somebody to go over it with me. I didn't
> even know what I was doing sometimes. I go, how do you do
> this? How do you do this?

Exclusion, as felt by Elena, had the quality of not being chosen, being left out. Describing a group lesson about differences between writing styles and her difficulty in understanding the lesson, Elena concluded, "(the teacher) was going to choose who she was going to get the
message across to and those of us who didn't understand were left out."

Teacher attitudes about and toward students resonated within the
classroom walls and created images of invisibility. People expressed a
lack of care toward them on the part of teachers. Eduardo indicated
that "nobody seemed to notice if I was there or not. The teachers didn't
seem to care."

Comparing the community center where she was attending a social event, Juanita said, "The community center here cares and encour-
ages us. They understand the lives we live. I didn't have that in the education program I went to." The importance of a community of care and
assistance was a major thread in the individual accounts whether in describing their everyday lives or as an element that was missing in educational situations.

Judith's description of an adult learning experience indicates her
lack of interest and enthusiasm for situations that make her feel
invisible.

> I lost interest in the class I was in. They gave you a book, said,
> do this, and put you in a corner and put you on your own.
> They acted as if we weren't even there.

The third dimension of marginality, inferior status, also conveyed a sense of anger and justified indignation at the discrimination people experienced. People felt inferior due to comments and actions of both teachers and peers. Speaking about peer attitudes of non-Hispanic students Olivia stated:

> They're the ones that made me feel inferior to them because a lot of them (Anglos) were making it. I don't know, like now, how I would feel if someone was to tell me hey-you know, there's this class you can come and take. The majority of the girls are white, but there'll be, you know, a few Spanish girls in there.

Olivia's willingness to give a program a chance appears to be impaired due to her past adult experiences of humiliation and the pain she remembered. Bertha described her experiences with discrimination and struggle in the following way.

> The class lasted eight weeks, and most of us were all out of there by the third day because everybody was so discouraged, so messed up. From the very first day [the teacher] kept saying this, like, "Let's see, how can I get through to your kind of people." She didn't come out and tell us "it's you brown people" but she could sure say it another way, and it meant the same thing.

Not only bias, but blatant racism conveyed through disrespect, difference, and put-downs is part of the educational reality for Chicanos/as as they attempt to engage in efforts of learning and skill upgrade.

Learning Expectations

Chicanos/as are looking for learning environments that support their cultural norms. The learning endeavor is serious business, and people have expectations about the conditions and atmosphere that ought to exist. Learner expectations about the educational environment extend beyond how Chicanos/as are treated by teachers and peers, yet are influenced very specifically by their perceptions of teacher and peer behavior. Several dimensions were evidenced, such as classroom environment, program organization, and the teaching-learning exchange.

Criticisms of teachers in controlling the learning environment and setting the learning agenda, as well as of the teaching-learning exchange, reflect these individuals' strong desire to learn, rather than their total rejection of the idea of the teacher or the value of programs. Likewise, there is a legitimacy placed on the knowledge offered.

Aspects of the classroom environment that were important to people included the learning atmosphere, the ambiance of the setting, and the decorum of classroom routines. Individuals recounted noisy classrooms where it was difficult to engage in serious study. Some blamed the teachers for not calming things down and creating a more serious atmosphere. Some suggested that students needed to take more responsibility in creating a learning environment, but all indicated a lack of enthusiasm for programs where learning was not taken seriously. Environmental aspects greatly influenced whether or not people stuck with a program.

Cecilia's ideas about the classroom environment pointed to not only what she finds to be a conducive environment for learning, but also exhibited her attitudes about other learners as well as the role of teachers. Talking about the classroom environment, she put it this way:

> The people that were there weren't interested. They were just there messing around and making people laugh. You really couldn't get into it. The teachers didn't make them calm down or anything.

For Cecilia to feel comfortable that she will profit from her efforts, certain criteria within the environment will need to be present.

Questioning the lack of organization within programs, Patricia suggests that the level of quality that exists in some adult education programs does not meet her expectations as a learner.

> They don't keep up with you. I know they have a lot of work, but we students always had to keep bugging them and bugging them. Half the time, they don't know where your records are. It seems to be hard for them. When you first go in to register, they kinda like don't know where to put you, and after you're done filling out all that paperwork—they've lost you. And by that time, you don't want to really go through all this.

Emotionally, this disorganization is perceived as demeaning and disrespectful of one's time. Sylvia experienced program confusion and disorganization differently. Her assessment of the teacher in the follow-ing statement creates the image of a friendly but ineffective learning encounter.

> They were friendly, but they weren't too helpful because, I don't know, maybe because there were too many people in the classroom or something.

While a friendly environment may be helpful in making people feel comfortable and welcome, in the end, most people look for teacher as-sistance in a well-planned program.

A final dimension of learning expectations is the concept of shar-ing knowledge, the exchange of information between teachers and learners. People thought teachers should have a responsibility to teach in a way so they would and could learn. In addition, individuals indi-cated they expected teachers to share the knowledge they have. Olivia explained it this way.

> It was an Anglo lady that directed the whole class. She was the one that offered the program, and she made everybody in there feel so stupid. Since she was teaching, how are we sup-posed to know until we've been taught. She should give us an example. First, like she asked us this question, and we didn't know the answer so she explained it like in "terms" but didn't give us any examples, and nobody's catching on. I stood up and asked her. I says, "Could you give me an example of what you mean?" She couldn't, or wouldn't, saying if she did that she would be giving us the answer.

Teachers withholding of information and knowledge contributed to Olivia's feelings of being stupid, while at the same time reinforced the notion that the educational apparatus and, more importantly, the teachers, regulated who learns what and who has access to what knowledge.

Sandra cited a teacher's teaching style that she perceived to inter-fere with the exchange of information and learning. The centrality of the teacher in the learning environment is pointed out again in the fol-lowing statement. Sandra's experiences, however, focus on the impor-tance of the learner. There is a sense of being ignored as the learner and needing to fit in to an already defined teaching style.

> It was a group. See she would go to different subjects. I got in-volved right in the middle of the session or whatever, and she

was going to algebra when I don't even know division. Well she was already on algebra, and she wouldn't stop the class to get back to me. She was on algebra, and then went back to fractions, and then the next day we were on reading and then the following day we would be on a different subject. It was all mixed up where we were going. That's another reason why I couldn't really get anywhere.

People take seriously the notion of responsible teaching. Teachers have an obligation toward the student to share their knowledge in an orderly environment with the needs of the students in mind. What people are asking for, and expect, is a learner-centered exchange. Patricia stated, "They weren't teaching me anything. They were teaching me the way they wanted, not the way that would help me. I never learned to read."

Intercultural Understanding

Cultural pride is a strong theme running throughout the texts. It is a way of being, a way of knowing, and a way of belonging. Individuals had to contend with affronts to their ethnic heritage and backgrounds, and their sense of difference was questioned rather than valued. Images of the "Other" created by program mechanisms and structures spotlight their "Otherness." Dimensions of intercultural understanding include notions of cultural identity and use of their native language, Spanish.

Cultural identity is carried around inside and is worn on the outside. Silence regarding one's racial and ethnic identity is perceived as disrespect. Judith's indignation reveals the strength of her convictions and the importance of her culture. Her statements suggest that intercultural understanding is an important criteria in the selection of adult programs.

You never forget what you are no matter how white the world is. You are a Chicano and that's all there is to it. My ethnic background was pushed aside like I was supposed to forget about it.

I would have felt more comfortable with more Chicanos around, because I would have figured they've come from the same background as I have. What makes me uncomfortable is why does it always have to be a white teacher? That's what I don't like.

As a result of the breakdown in cultural respect, Judith has become uncomfortable with the idea of Anglo teachers in programs that serve large numbers of Chicanos/as. Being unable to relate to another's background and heritage, one's ethnic culture, economic class, or gender is seen as a problem.

Olivia related an experience that she had to contend with in a racist classroom as she was pursuing her educational goals. Olivia reported her retort to the teacher's comments. "I got frustrated in one class and the teacher said, 'You Chicanos are known for being hot-tempered people." I go, "You've never seen a white lady mad or a black woman? What are you trying to throw at me?'" Being defined as different and lesser than others, she resisted the stereotype that the teacher used to represent her.

Language is an important, some believe significant, element of cultural identity. None of the individuals in this study were monolingual Spanish; a few were monolingual English. For those individuals who speak both Spanish and English, language is a way to move from one world to the other. Yet, individuals were told they must remove themselves from the context of their history and their everyday cultural realities. Cristina related that they were told they could not speak Spanish, to leave it outside the adult education classroom door.

> [The teachers] told us to leave our Spanish outside the classroom. I tell my son it's good to speak two languages—bilingual—try to speak your own language not only just English. They shouldn't make us feel bad about our language.

This practice is a common complaint that I heard from many people, and it is also something I have witnessed in traditional adult learning centers, especially those with large numbers of Hispanics, and in many English as a Second Language (ESL) classrooms where multiple ethnic and racial groups participate. The logic of the requirement to leave the native language at the door is said to be that it is more difficult to learn English if individuals switch back and forth between languages. Anyone who has learned anther language knows that a process of translating back and forth occurs naturally and may even be necessary in order to learn the new language. Forbidding this practice, at least the verbalizing process, inside the classroom strips people of their identity. It may also hinder acquisition of English.

There is a high value, among Chicanos/as, placed on being bilingual, and their children are encouraged to learn both Spanish and English. Situations were recounted where bilingual skills were not respected and people were made to feel badly about their native language. As a kid in school, Eduardo may have had to put up with ridicule, but as an adult in adult education programs he feels he has other options. Environments that do not respect language fluency and skill levels are not safe environments.

> If teachers make me feel uncomfortable about my English, I leave. Some teachers are so bad. As a kid you have no choice. If it's that bad now, I leave.

Along with language, knowing one's own history creates a sense of place in the larger social world. There is a longing for Chicano history in the curriculum of adult programs. Curriculum that reflects the lives of Chicano/a individuals represents respect for their contributions to history. Omission signifies exclusion and invisibility for many individuals. Problems associated with absence of one's history were pointed out by these comments of Margaret and Jose.

> I wish I knew more about my history, where I come from. If I had been closer to my grandmother, I probably would have learned more about my heritage. Now I wish I would have. Why don't they include that in adult courses? (Margaret)

> After all this time, we are said to belong to a minority culture. We even see enemies among other Hispanics, and this is all because of ignorance and a lack of information about our culture, our plight. (Jose)

These individuals know a great deal about available educational options in their communities. As people attempt to upgrade their education, there is continual conflict between what they must give up, or sacrifice, as part of the educational contract and what they can hope to gain. As adults who have been unsuccessful in achieving academic credentials and struggling against the dominant discourse that represents them as outsiders and failures, individuals continue to negotiate their cultural identities and to look for educational experiences that are grounded in concepts of justice that grant them respect.

Similarities Between Education Experiences as a Youth and as an Adult

The adult education programs people described and their experiences are reminiscent of their childhood experiences, particularly the junior high and high school experiences presented earlier. Furthermore, these similarities appear to be factors that influence people's continuing efforts and/or decisions as they determine how best to satisfy their educational needs and desires. Three factors were characterized when the stories between adult educational experiences were compared with youth educational experiences including: teacher attitudes, academic quality, and cultural respect (see table 5.1).

Teachers' Attitudes

Adult education experiences highlighted the attitudes of teachers as a lack of care and attention and positioned teachers as a central concern in these educational encounters. Adult experiences are more graphically detailed with particular incidents in mind, whereas youth experiences give the sense of a more general, pervasive lack of care on the part of teachers that seems to have colored the memories of those years. Since there was such a generalized experience of teacher disinterest during the younger years, it may be difficult to remember specific incidents, but the sense or feelings that people still hold about their younger educational years reflect the power of the memories and the images.

As youth, individuals described teacher attitudes as playing an important role in their academic success. Lack of learning assistance, academic guidance, and teaching instruction were voiced as the difference in attention they received compared to Anglo youth. Adult experiences of insensitive teacher attitudes are emotionally felt as exclusion and marginalization. Teachers walked away from them and exhibited direct racist behavior. In their youth experiences, individuals reported feeling that inappropriate teacher attitudes had a similar emotional effect, but were described more as a sense of being ignored by teachers. In both cases, we get a picture of individual needs and differences not being taken into account, which results in people feeling invisible and disconnected in the schooling environments.

Factors	Youth Experiences	Adult Experiences
Teacher Attitudes	Breakdown of trust Lack of care and attention Put-downs Racism Little academic assistance	Lack of care/neglect Invisibility Racism Little academic assistance Exclusion Inferior status
Academic Quality	Tracking into working/lower-class jobs Disregard for individual goals Non-challenging courses Reliance on attendance vs. abilities Educational differentials	Disorganization of programs Withholding of knowledge Poor teaching Disregard for individual goals Knowledgeable agents Isolated learning
Cultural Respect	Discrimination Punishment for speaking Spanish Lack of respect for difference	Discrimination Disregard for first language Subordination of culture

Table 5.1
Similarities Between Chicano/a Education Experiences as a Youth and as an Adult

The breakdown of trust between youth and their teachers appears to have resulted due to teachers not legitimizing the knowledge individuals have about their own lives. Teachers did not believe Julia or Jimmy when they asked for help with the gangs that were harassing them at their schools nor did the teachers believe that Cecilia could do more advanced math, which was of more interest to her. Those who were intimidated by racial remarks could trust the teachers to mistreat them and learned who to stay away from.

Trust, as it relates to adult educational experiences, was also noted; however, it was categorized as a factor that was taken into account in terms of academic quality. They learned to mistrust teachers who ignored them and did not share their knowledge. Trust was also broken when teachers did not take into account differing learning styles or cognitive experiences.

Both youth and adult experiences record the racism that pervades the lives of these individuals. As adults, this is experienced as being put in an inferior status, while as youth, they remember the put-downs that were used to maintain low self-esteem. Generally, teachers in both adult and youth education exhibited similar ideologies in terms of dealing with these Chicano/a individuals with similar results; individuals walked away from situations that did not affirm or respect their cultural identity nor supported their educational needs and desires.

Academic Quality

As youth, individuals reported being tracked into lower-level classes; none of the people indicated they were on the college track. Their educational goals and desires, as a result, were not taken into consideration, and several statements regarding low-level courses, e.g., extra gym classes, chorus, drama, and home economics, were described. In addition to the experiences of being tracked into working and lower-class jobs, individuals remembered not getting the same level of service that they saw others getting, especially as it related to guidance and counseling.

As adults, there were similar reflections within the context of adult responsibilities and commitments. Linear programs starting where one left off were questioned as being appropriate for all individuals. Specific course content was challenged as well if it did not meet educational goals. Individuals perceive they know a great deal about their educational needs and desires, and many felt there was a general disregard for their perceived goals.

Questioning the quality of academic choices offered to individuals both as youth and as adults indicated that people have an awareness of the limited options that are presented to them and have expectations that they deserve better. Resisting both the limited range of choices and the poor quality of programs suggests a lack of trust in the dominant educational enterprise, at least for themselves and their ethnic cultural group.

Attendance issues as played against academic abilities are related by individuals as important in their youth education. Attendance policy is used to exclude individuals from participating in classes and isolates them from the general school population. It is also used to manipulate behavior and force compliance. It is about control, not about teaching and learning. Isolated, individualized learning situations, as documented by adult education experiences, appear to achieve the same result by pushing people to the margins of the learning community. Learning is a social enterprise for Chicanos/as, as well as many other groups, yet individualized teaching strategies ignore even the dominant literature that talks of the social nature of learning.

Individuals reported their adult education experiences as including disorganized programs and poor teaching skills. The impact on people of such disorganization and untrained teachers signifies to them that, according to the dominant discourse, they do not deserve any better. The rejection of these programs signals a problem in the type of programs that are offered. The underfunding of adult basic education and English literacy programs is a pretty clear indication of the low status of such programs, of those for whom they are designed, and, by inference, the people who participate in them.

Questions about the academic quality in all educational programs whether at the youth or the adult level indicate a resistance to inadequate programs at various stages of one's life. Required by law to provide public education, whether for those under or over twenty-one, public school systems and adult education divisions do not take seriously the effect that low-quality programs have on individual interest, commitment, and learning. People expect equitable access to education and comparable quality of programs that the dominant white, middle-class communities get. They believe they deserve more than what they've been getting.

Cultural Respect

Accounts of discrimination based on race and ethnicity are well documented in the texts of individuals in this study. Lack of respect for differences as identified in people's youth experiences are recounted in adult education programs as a disregard for one's culture. In both cases, there is a general sense that one ought to push cultural identity to one side—or leave it outside the classroom door—without being upset about it.

People reported language discrimination in both adult and youth educational experiences. The actual form this treatment took varied. Many adults recounted their efforts to learn English and the struggles they confronted including outright punishment. As adult learners, people experience a general disregard for their first language. Punishment is more subtle and takes the form of making people feel uncomfortable about their language. Reports of not speaking Spanish in front of Anglos can be seen as a result of ridicule and witnessed as general disrespect for one's culture.

Other forms of discrimination experienced in adult education programs was a lack of multicultural curriculum that included the history of Mexican Americans. Individuals did not criticize the materials that were in the learning centers, only that there were no materials that represented their lives. Accounts of youth education included being taught Spanish from a book of irrelevant stories rather than the everyday contextual conversations of their lives. Student subjectivity was not included in the classroom curriculum and was experienced as discriminatory and demeaning.

The demand for cultural respect in learning encounters suggests that individuals expect intercultural understanding. Likewise, if respect is not present in these learning encounters, there is little interest in continued participation. In summary, the experiences of these adults, in both adult education programs and youth education, present factors that are taken into account when making decisions about the appropriate actions to take in furthering one's academic skills. Differentials in teacher attitudes, academic quality, and cultural respect restrict access to acceptable educational opportunities.

Program Deficiencies

The notion of "second chance" programs is still in vogue. What this means for adults who participate in adult basic education and English literacy is that it is a second chance for programs to reproduce the same situations, standards, and results that have been offered before. In other words, we are "giving" adults another chance to fail.

The concrete situations, the details of lived experiences, indicate that some adult education programs do not provide a conducive environment for individuals to learn. It is not to suggest that all adult education programs are the same. There are, no doubt, examples of programs better able to serve the needs of Chicanos/as as well as programs less able to serve this population. Compatibility between cultural values and dominant educational ideology does seem to be in conflict, however. Individual choices appear restricted if solely focused on traditional programs.

The practices of adult education conflict with the ethic of care and assistance that people both value and seek. For example, individualized self-paced instruction, which enables easier tracking of student progress and time expended for institutional accountability, although a prominent method of instructional delivery, denies satisfaction of the felt need for cooperative learning and sharing of resources. Those who have experienced adult programs that utilize individual instruction, conclude they are being neglected and invisible and, in some cases, not chosen. The notion of marginalization also includes a sense of anger and justified indignation suggesting that different instructional models may be more effective.

The centrality of teachers is clearly documented in the stories the people presented here. The educational system, whether at the youth or adult level, espouses a system of difference. The teachers carry the ideology through their attitudes and actions. Teaching strategies, particularly self-directed learning and its reliance on individualized self-paced learning with its privatizing effects on learners (Collins 1995), mechanisms such as classroom organization, the hidden adult literacy curriculum (Quigley and Holsinger 1993), and the discourse of the "Other" with its cultural putdowns, discounting, and racist talk all conspire to reproduce the status quo of inequality and hostile learning environments. A commodified system of difference within adult education contributes significantly to social control mechanisms.

This study did not report whether teachers are aware of their failure to educate Chicano/a students in adult programs (Montero-Sieburth 1990). Certainly there are teachers who are more sensitive. In the observational field notes, there are accounts of adult education teachers who talked with each other about the difficulties Chicano/a students were having in one program. Yet they blame the failure of the students on the students' culture and the students' own lack of motivation. The teachers expect Chicano/a students to assimilate. The assimilation perspective reflects the belief that ethnic groups should adapt to the dominant culture; therefore, it would be inappropriate to teach them about their history or culture. Baker (1996) suggests that teachers do not have the academic skills necessary to meet the academic and social needs of Chicano/a students.

The unmet learning expectations these individuals have of adult programs suggest other structural mechanisms and practices of schooling where access to knowledge is regulated through the teaching/learning exchange by either unskilled teachers, disorganized programs, or classroom environments where teaching and learning are not taken seriously. The dimensions of these inadequate educational settings, as described by participants, contribute to the marginalization they feel. This notion is reinforced by the double bind situation described in educational experiences. As youth, individuals look to the institution of education to further their economic and social needs and desires in order to participate in, and contribute to, mainstream life, yet they reject particular settings due to perceived discrimination and subordination.

The lack of intercultural understanding is again reminiscent of previous experiences where individuals are defined as the "Other." The monolingual educational settings, the omission within the curriculum materials of the many historical contributions by Chicanos/as, and the predominance of middle-class Anglo instructors suggests individuals must forget who they are and strive for the dominant culture espoused in adult programs. Further, people identified characteristics of intercultural understanding and marginalization as similar to their subjective experiences in other areas of social life as well as in the political and economic realms of everyday life.

Since none of the individuals were enrolled in adult education programs during the course of this study, it must be recognized that *people left programs* they found to be inappropriate for them. Having engaged in adult education programs at some point during adulthood, these individuals challenge the image that adults with low-level English literacy skills are uninterested in learning.

The individuals here are reaffirming their cultural pride and values of relatedness, sharing, cooperation, and community by voicing their concerns about programs that do not support their values. They are not rejecting education nor the knowledge that they can gain. These are individuals who have walked away from programs that did not meet their educational needs nor sustain their cultural identities. Supportive of this notion of culture as action is Dirlik's (1987) critique of culture as an emancipatory possibility. Chicanos/as view their culture as dynamic and rooted in traditions that are evolving and sustaining. They use their cultural values to guide their decisions and actions.

Mexican Americans and other disenfranchised groups cannot afford to enroll in programs that do not meet their needs. It is imperative that our educational structures and practices in formal programs become more responsive and supportive of people with differing social, economic, political, gender, and cultural backgrounds who look to adult education to assist them in reaching their educational goals.

Chapter 6

Cultural Actions, Tactical Choices

A tactical choice born of a prudent awareness of the balance
of power. (Scott 1990, 183)

Seeking out adult education programs is but one course of cultural
action that some individuals pursued as they attempted to meet their
self-identified learning needs. Additional actions of resistance and production unmask the connections of the past with the present. Remembering past injustices and discrimination related to learning and education, people formulate responses that honor their values and priorities.
In the end, however, the level of gain may be minute focused as it is on
incremental individual gain. Mexican Americans battle against a society organized around race and class that continues to attempt to exclude them. Recognizing the odds, Maria, Olivia, Jose, Carlos, Patricia,
and the others devise mechanisms, sometimes successfully, sometimes
unsuccessfully, which will further their learning needs and desires. The
reasons people have for continued learning and education provides a
grounding, or foundation, for their subsequent actions.

A typology of strategies depicting the responses individuals created to counter their marginal status within the dominant culture and to attain educational and social equality was developed based on the themes that emerged from the individual stories. The criterion used in drawing up the typology is the manner in which individuals related to the dominant discourse of the relationship between their minority status and the importance of educational credentials. The two polar possibilities are acts of refusal to engage in the mainstream culture at one extreme, and the creation of learning opportunities at the other. Between these two are a variety of other strategies of resistance and production.

Why Persist?

The instrumental importance of an education, such as acquiring specific technical skills, is well embedded in the dominant discourse through promotion of global competition and the subsequent need for new or higher-level skills at the individual level. While a number of people believe higher-level skills will get them a better job, there were varying degrees of trust that the dominant enterprise of education will, in fact, do that. For some, there is a degree of hope that better skills will lead them out of the aches and pains of manual labor. People perceive an advantage to having certain skills, both academic and vocational, however, the specific reasons given often varied. They talked of wanting to get better jobs, to build self-esteem, and/or to affirm one's cultural identity.

The need to build self-esteem, as a reason for wanting higher-level skills, recognizes the toll that educational exclusion and discrimination has had on one's self-concept as well as acknowledges the importance of the self in the educational process. Individuals voicing these desires recall repeated incidents of "put-downs" and challenges to their academic abilities by teachers, administrators, and peers. Perceived notions of being less than someone else, and settling for something less than what one wanted or desired, are evident. Affirmations of cultural identity emerged from participant texts. Images of courage and stamina were depicted as individual stories documented the struggles of getting an education through phrases and words like "put up with" and "sticking it out." People construct and reconstruct social cultural identity based on contradictions and conflicting experiences. How people come to see themselves and who they are is either challenged or reaffirmed through interaction with social institutions. The dialectic of the individual/society gets played out in social identity (re)formation and (re)-construction, a continual back and forth interplay. Acquiring skills and knowledge through learning and education is a key component to identity.

These men and women can be considered undereducated, as well as unserved, by the dominant educational system. By their own descriptions, they indicate educational needs in specific literacy areas such as reading comprehension, spelling, pronunciation of certain words, writing skills, and math. There were also some who desired vocational skill training but saw their low academic skills as stumbling blocks. There were others who focused on the "piece of paper" more so than the level of skills they may or may not have. Included in people's testimonies were statements of desires to upgrade skills, regret at not "sticking it out," and determination to reach certain goals. Cecilia told me, "I probably can get where I want to, if I want to now," but she recognizes that she would have to deal with the way some people think about her class or culture. "I would have to deal with [it] and they would have to deal with [it] as well. That's basically it." On the other hand, she stated, "Then again, I'll never become manager or an owner of a business. It's a real hard thing to do, but my opportunities are whatever I make of them."

The tensions and contradictions evident in Cecilia's statement represent the constraints and dilemmas Chicanos/as attempt to deal with as they confront the realities of their lives. Cecilia acknowledges, however, that she has rights and reasonable expectations of being given a chance to prove herself; in other words, "They would have to deal with it as well." If in fact "opportunities are whatever I make of them," then the stories of Olivia, Carlos, Maria, Patricia, and Jose (and others) reminding us of the difficulty of getting an education if one is a Chicano/a, might not carry the weight that they do. For some, anger at opportunities taken from them is evident in their stories. Olivia tells of the numerous manual labor jobs she must take as a result of not completing school whereas she wanted to have a professional career.

> There's so many intelligent Chicano people, and why are they not up there doing the same thing? Just like myself—I could have been up there doing a lot of this stuff but because

I didn't have that little piece of paper, they took that (opportunity) away from me. I wanted to do something like teaching or counseling.

The action one takes as a response to historical and contemporary
experiences of struggle, discrimination, and difference can take many
forms.

Cultural Action

Cultural action (Freire 1985) describes the actions taken by people
when they realize they have been exploited and subordinated to an inferior status, when they realize they deserve more, and when they demand justice. As knowledgeable actors, people assert themselves
through strategic action to advance their own interests.

The level of knowing can vary, but coming to know is based on reflecting on one's own life history and the history of the group. Individuals walked away from educational institutions they found to be unsafe,
inferior, and uncaring. As adults, their educational needs and desires
persist. The majority of people used a range of actions to try and meet
those unmet needs; they recounted efforts of looking for alternatives
where too few choices exist.

Practices of Resistance and Production

Strategies of resistance and production indicate a range of action
moving along a continuum from an almost total refusal of buying into
the dominant discourse of educational credentials and skills, to the op-
posite end of creating opportunities to learn self-identified and other
identified skills and abilities. The kinds of responses illustrated here are
not exhaustive or mutually exclusive. People employed a number of
strategies either simultaneously or successively over the course of
adulthood. Obviously, only the strategies people reported can be included in this discussion, but we can probably assume they employed a
wider range of actions.

Acts of Refusal

When asked about efforts to upgrade skills, several individuals indicated they had never thought about enrolling in adult education programs to meet the need of improving academic or vocational skills and had no desire to participate in any type of educational program. They were aware that programs were available. Several different dimensions were identified in this group of actions. Typical of this type of resistance was a reliance on cultural roles, such as Cristina's statement about her priorities. "I never needed to go back to school. My husband always worked and I raised our daughter. She's older now and left the house, but now I'm taking care of my grandmother. I just never thought about it." Cristina described herself as being able to read and write well enough for her purposes, although she indicated she was still uncomfortable with math. She definitively stated she was not interested in academics.

Juanita, who worked in a drug store for seventeen years, expressed another perspective indicative of this resisting practice. "I have no interest in school or anything like that. I worked for the drug store seventeen years. I don't need a GED or high school diploma. If you do a good job, it doesn't seem like it should make any difference." Juanita, like some others, separates knowing from academic credentials. Her pragmatic view of coupling skills with job requirements suggests she sees education for what it can do for her rather than education as an end in itself.

A longing for justice, to be judged by who one is and the job one does, was also reflected in these comments by men who have jobs, albeit not necessarily the jobs they want.

> I know enough to do my job. I'm always there. I help the Mexican customers. There's no reason for me to get a GED. If they would put me in road sales maybe, but I don't want to sit in school anyway. (Tony)

> Having a diploma really don't have anything to do with it. You have to first build your reputation and, you know, I'm a upright guy I'm trying to keep my life together here. It has to do with your attitude and your personality. (Carlos)

Both men indicate lack of need as well as lack of desire to give the educational enterprise another chance. Jose's perspective added another dimension to acts of refusal as a strategy to challenge the marginal educational status and the dominant system. Along with recognition of the discrimination he has experienced is a sense of anger and a subsequent response of almost total refusal. Recall his words:

> I always had cheap paying jobs, nothing that was going to get me anywhere. The opportunities weren't there after dropping out. A diploma wouldn't help though. Most employers like to give the jobs to the Anglos first.

Supportive of Jose's perspective is Maria's refusal to engage in adult education programs even though she cannot read or write English. She remembers experiences of humiliation at the hands of Anglos, ridiculing her for her broken English. Prior to the days of knowing much English, she was sure people were talking about her, which made her feel incompetent and stupid. Refusing to get involved with schooling, there is a distinction between learning and schooling that keeps some away from engaging in dominant culture institutions.

Maria's refusal to take advantage of educational services for which she is eligible sustains her inability to move around comfortably in her community. At the same time, however, monitoring her environment, she relies on the literacy skills of others. Nevertheless, Maria's testimony documents her struggle, at one point saying, "I can't do it. I can't read. Help me." The contradictions of Maria's conflicting perspective and actions indicate some degree of control over her life, however, the consequences continue to limit her choices. The trade-off for Maria is that she is able to maintain her cultural identity and values, her community and sense of belonging. She has found ways to adjust.

Acts of refusal to engage in adult education programs were characterized by multiple perspectives including a reliance on cultural roles, the belief that one's economic worth should not be defined by one's educational level, and by the knowledge that the color of one's skin means more than a "piece of paper." Perspectives based on past experiences, beliefs about what is right and just, and values informed by history and culture that all lead to action, support the notion that action is situated in time and space as a continuous flow of conduct. Equally evident is a prudent awareness by people of the system of inequalities and their place within the system.

Avoidance

Proceeding across the continuum is the category of avoidance as a strategy of resistance. Avoidance suggests staying away from a place that is unpleasant, uncomfortable, even racist. Numerous individuals spoke of staying away from certain programs within the community citing unhelpful teachers, uncaring environments, high costs, and boring programs.

Avoidance begins to uncover the fact that a majority of people in this study (75 percent) have participated in adult education programs in the past. Since individuals were neither enrolled in programs nor had graduated from programs during the time of the study, it suggests that individuals found adult education programs that they had participated in to be unsatisfactory. People who enroll in programs but leave prior to completion are often considered dropouts of adult education. Another view suggests individuals walk away from learning situations that are not supportive of their educational goals and cultural values. They are pushed out by uncaring, ineffective, and hostile teachers and administrators, and by alienating structures such as teaching practices, academic tracking, linear program models that require students to progress from one point to another, and bureaucratic "red tape."

Word of mouth is a reliable tool that people use in making decisions and, in fact, is sought out when trying to locate educational services. Typical of the notion of avoidance are statements of hesitation informed by previous experiences of ineffective teaching and unmet expectations. According to Reuben:

> Word of mouth works both ways. We share information with our family and friends. If it is a bad program, we say stay away.

Elena related her experiences of an adult education program that was not supportive of her educational agenda. "I lost interest in the class I was in. They gave you a book, said do this, and put you in a corner on your own. They acted as if we weren't even there." Tied to the lack of assistance Elena felt she wanted, is also the notion of being made to feel invisible. She indicated that she would have to think about whether or not she would attend another program in the future.

> I don't know. I know I won't go back there. It was a waste of
> my time because I like to get some help. I haven't thought
> about finding another program.

A large number of study participants indicated hesitation in following through on thoughts and longings to upgrade their skills. Several comments suggestive of a "wait-and-see" stance were evident. For
Larry, "I'd have to see what it would be like," and for Eduardo, "It depends on who the people are." As a result, neither Larry nor Eduardo
are seeking out programs.

Olivia seems to support this notion, but her attitude is more personal based on not just her past experiences as a youth but also remembering her experiences as an adult.

> I don't know, like now. I really don't know how I feel if some-
> one was to tell me, hey, you know, there's this class you can
> come and take it. The majority of the girls there are white,
> but there'll be a few Spanish girls in there, or I just go and find
> that out, I don't know.

> You're supposed to train us and teach us. You know I wanted
> that certificate ten years ago. I probably would have gone
> back to school, but see, there again, it happened the same
> way. Nobody wanted to take the time even after all these
> years. So I haven't changed my mind. I still feel, to a certain
> degree, cheated—but you know how I can make up for it is, it
> will never happen to my kids.

Olivia's sense of being cheated in the past influences decisions
made in the present. Her uncertainty about educational opportunities
today are overshadowed by her unmet expectations in the teaching-learning exchange of the past. As evidenced in her story, Olivia's
anger at losing out is embedded in educational experiences that included lack of cultural respect by teachers and peers, academic discrimination related to her Spanish literacy and low-level English skills, and
struggles to get quality education for her children. Such negative experiences coalesce in her hesitation and ultimate reluctance to engage in
adult education programs. Her negative experiences, in the process, inform her beliefs about what she must do to protect her children.
Knowing how dominant culture institutions work, she is clear that she
must help her children get through the system.

Olivia goes on to say,

> I'd have to go back so far I don't want to anymore. See I can't
> just jump in where I want now. Why can't I just take a few
> classes in what I'm good at? Why do I have to backtrack all
> the way to where they want me to get a GED?

Olivia also knows that the system of schooling has its own logic of
linear development that she wants to avoid. As she sees it, there is no
way for her to take a few classes that interest her because of her lack of a
high school diploma, and she does not want what the system tells her
she needs, namely a GED.

Racial discrimination in adult education programs was documented in numerous stories. Discriminatory comments and actions by
adult educators are to be avoided at all costs. Recall Olivia's adult education class experience.

> I got frustrated in one class, and the teacher said, "You Chi-
> canos are known for being hot tempered people." I go, "You
> never seen a white lady mad or a black woman? What are you
> trying to throw at me?" Most of the Chicana women only
> went for about three weeks.

Avoidance as a resisting practice ensures protection of one's cultural identity and beliefs about oneself. Affirmation of identity has not
been the experience in most educational institutions. Hesitation based
on past discriminatory encounters, a "wait-and-see" attitude, and dis-
appointment in the teaching-learning exchange of adult efforts, indicate adults who have not found a supportive environment to meet their
educational needs.

As a counter to being cheated out of an education and made to feel
less than others through challenges by teachers and administrators
concerning their academic abilities, individuals reported extensive efforts both educationally and noneducationally to get what they need in
order to succeed. There were numerous accounts of exclusion, marginalization, lack of care, and unfulfilled learning expectations. Patricia
reflected to me, "This was the first time I've really contemplated how
hard it is to get an education." As a strategy of resistance to the status
quo, however, they continue to walk away from programs due to unfulfilled expectations of finding quality, respectful, and caring adult
programs.

Alternatives

Finding alternatives as a strategy of resistance takes the form of looking at and trying out various educational options that might assist individuals in reaching their educational goals. Some individuals countered programs that are discriminatory and unsatisfactory by walking away and looking for alternatives. The knowledge people have about their needs and available options prompts some to keep searching for programs of instructional quality and human, intercultural respect. Exploring options and searching for quality adult education programs suggest people are looking for opportunities where their needs and desires for both education and affirmation of cultural identity can be met. Alternatives described by people include considerations of compatible philosophies of education and human interaction.

Carlos views academic credentials as required criteria for securing a good job. He recounted his repeated attempts to secure enough credits to graduate from high school prior to reaching the age of twenty-one, the official cutoff age for serving individuals under secondary education funding. Having left school at the age of sixteen because of his so-called troublemaking and the school's discriminatory practices, he went to three other programs but subsequently left each one. He attended the district alternative high school, moved to another town one hundred fifty miles away and attended an adult night school completion program and, finally, returned to his hometown community to attend another high school within his local school district. At the age of twenty-one, he had not completed school and he reported,

> I liked going to school, it's just the way I got treated a lot of times. I didn't get the respect from people. I was ignored a lot of the time, so I didn't give them the respect. The jocks got all the attention. Other students, they put down.

In his twenties, without a diploma, he has taken a different approach. His strategy to deal with his uncompleted education was to focus on proving one's self by character versus educational credentials that the dominant discourse equates with success. There is a level of conflicted knowing, however, in Carlos's recognition that in the end a diploma does not guarantee getting a good job.

> They like somebody with an education. A lot of places you can't get a job if you don't have a diploma or anything. It's

just hard. Sometimes I've filled out on job applications that
yeah I do have a high school [diploma]. I've filled that out for
better chances, but I guess that really don't have nothing to
do with it.

Angelina's search for a good job through educational advancement is similar to Carlos's. During the twenty-six years since she left
school at the age of sixteen, Angelina had attended three different
adult education programs. Each program had differing characteristics.
One program housed at a local church was staffed by volunteers and located in her local community, another was a large adult vocational center in the downtown area of her city, and the third was an adult night
program in an elementary school. Relating her experience at the night
program where she wanted to work on basic skills, Angelina said:

I want a good job where I can make money and I don't have
to work hard. So I've gone back a few times, but I never liked
the programs. You'd go to them for help, and they wouldn't
tell you how to figure it out or nothing. You figure it out yourself. I mean there are rude people and everything over there.
I just forgot about school.

She also reported starting a program in computers and got a certificate but was never able to use it.

I don't remember the year, but I went and got a certificate for
MS-DOS. It was like maybe seven or eight years ago, but I
don't even know anything about it now. They said I would
get a job with the training, but I never did.

In addition to how one is treated, the curriculum was a consideration in people's decisions about sticking with a particular program.
Sandra related her frustration with programs that would not let her
study the things she wanted.

I knew I needed math, that was OK, but I wanted to learn
more about how to put together business letters. They would
just give me this stuff about writing answers to questions. It
was like I had to do it their way. They didn't seem interested
in what I needed to learn.

Similar to Olivia who knew what she wanted to work on, "Why
can't I take what I want rather than starting all the way back to get the
GED?" Sandra protests the logic of adult basic education programs, but
unlike Olivia who now avoids adult programs, Sandra continues to look

for a program that can meet her needs as she defines them. Individuals clearly identified curriculum content and knowledge areas that they wanted to learn. As self-directed adult learners, they are interested in building and creating knowledge, not necessarily accumulating credentials, which stress passive acceptance of preselected knowledge and mechanisms of control. Because these learners do not have the required credentials, however, they feel restricted and are shut out of most vocational community college programs. The linear sequencing of credentialed degree programs does not fit the needs of many adult students who might simply want continuing education classes.

Alternative types of programs mentioned by study participants included community-based programs in community centers, churches, a women's center, and others located in local Chicano/a communities, adult night programs in public school facilities, adult basic education, GED and vocational programs at community college programs, and one-on-one tutoring in the home. Continuing education classes geared for those with lower academic skills could be added to the list. However, the key is that the alternatives that Chicanos/as seek must be culturally relevant. Instead they have found alternative models that still teach from a white, European perspective. This is not acceptable for many eligible adults.

Looking at alternatives, then, as a strategy to meet educational needs, encompasses finding a match between cultural philosophies and values of respect for the learner as knowledgeable agents in identifying their own needs and desires. It also signifies that there are standards of quality and intercultural interactions that individuals use as criteria in selecting certain programs that they will participate in over others that fall short of their standards. Finally, other alternatives, such as a reliance on one's character, can be viewed as a strategy of both resistance and production of meaning.

Preferences

Preferences as a strategy of resistance and production suggests the search for programs with particular features that are preferred over other features. As individuals reflected on the limited choices available in furthering education for themselves, numerous statements regarding preference in terms of programs were noted. Themes of care, assistance, and respect emerged from these collected statements. Focusing these themes into operational categories, the notions of tools and philosophies were developed. Preferences in philosophies included two categories: teachers attitudes and pedagogy. Preferences in educational tools contained references to instructional format, attendance policies, costs, materials, location, and safety issues.

Philosophical preferences in teacher attitudes reflected issues of cultural respect. The concern with teacher attitudes was well documented in the texts of study participants. The teacher held a central place in all recollections of past experiences, whether at the adult or youth level, and was the predominant concern in the consideration of potential programs that might be considered. Two variations of this concern were voiced. According to Eduardo, "Some teachers are so bad. As a kid, you have no choice. If it's that bad now, I leave." Whereas Margaret states, "I wouldn't worry about teachers now as an adult."

The concerns individuals have about teacher attitudes include beliefs they hold about adults as knowledgeable agents in the pursuit of their own learning, false beliefs regarding Chicanos/as and other Spanish-speaking groups, and biases including racism that are often exhibited by not only teachers but administrators of adult programs as well.

Many individuals voiced a desire for instructors who care about them and the lives they live. Reuben, Patricia, Elena, Jose, and many others look for teachers who care about individuals, especially those like themselves, people from other racial and class groups. Jose told me, "They have to want to spend time to help people, they have to communicate more, they have to give people recognition."

Philosophical preferences in pedagogy spotlight the importance of the adult as learner. Learning as a social process where people work together to gain and create knowledge is preferred to individualized, competitive, and isolated learning, which are reasons cited for leaving programs. Individuals reported teachers teaching to their own preferences and styles rather than the cultural preferences of students. Part of this notion focuses on the agenda and the style of the student over the agenda and the style of the teacher. Another important point here is that the self-paced approach that separates learners does not resonate with the culture of shared experience and relying on each other.

People are interested in gaining specific skills they have identified. They resist programs that do not reflect their interests and backgrounds and that do not acknowledge and build on the skills individuals bring with them to the classroom including social participation in communities and families, bilingual or biliteracy skills, and critical thinking skills used in everyday roles as parent, worker, citizen, and so on.

They expressed a desire for teachers who are knowledgeable and skillful at teaching. Individuals believe teachers should teach using knowledge of how adults in various cultures learn. There is also an expectation that since teachers are the ones who have the information, they have a responsibility to share and transmit that knowledge. Jose said, "Educated people have to want to give more." The teaching-learning exchange is an important factor in meeting educational needs.

Preferences in educational tools include items ranging from instructional format to location and safety issues. There appears to be a great deal of concern with individualized instruction and being left on one's own to figure things out. People recognize that the instructional format, as a tool to learning, is more effective when knowledge and skills are shared. Being left to work on one's own creates time delays and reinforces the sense of marginalization. There is a definite sense that they feel they are being punished when told to work on their own. People also complained of programs that waste their time through busy work and unfocused curriculum.

Attendance policies and issues of absences or "recycling of students," as one person named it, are not helpful in building relationships of trust, both important issues as documented from educational youth experiences. Adult programs that put heavy demands on attendance with penalties for a certain number of absences are not helpful to individuals who are trying to further their education. The ideology of these programs does not recognize the realities and commitments of everyday life.

Costs were brought up by several people. Statements centered on discriminatory preferential practices of social programs that pay for books and expenses for welfare recipients and at-risk youth, as well as people entering college who get scholarships and financial aid, while charging underemployed and working-class students fees that they cannot pay. Cristina related her concern that she had to pay for books and a program she had attended at one time, while she was aware that individuals who were on welfare and some younger adults who lived at a residential treatment center were allowed to attend free. "And us, we were paying more, we really wanted this. Why did we have to pay because we really wanted this?" Costs were also referred to in reference to changing class levels, moving from level three to level four for example, which requires different books and additional costs thus increasing costs for those on tight budgets.

Instructional materials used in most programs are not culturally sensitive, and they depict adult basic education students as lazy, in prison, on welfare, in court, having problems with parenting, and generally unable to cope with life. Dominant middle-class cultural values depicted in a lot of program materials and taught by teachers were viewed as "not our values." Some people asked for materials that would teach them more about their histories as indigenous peoples, suggesting preference for culturally relevant curriculum.

Finally, location and safety issues were identified as reasons for not attending certain programs. Some individuals who live in dangerous neighborhoods will not go out at night, while others identified specific neighborhoods to which they would not go. Several women also expressed preferences for programs that were more easily accessible due to their lack of transportation.

The preference of individuals suggest critical factors that are taken into account in the selection of programs. While variations exist, in general, there was potential interest in programs where individuals are treated with respect and regard and where their educational needs as identified by them are met in an environment of care.

Creating Opportunities for Learning

As people resist the marginalization and "Otherness" created by the dominant discourse of being "undereducated," individuals reported creative and varied approaches to creating opportunities for self-directed learning. Self-directed learning, in this case, focuses primarily on learning that takes place outside of formal educational settings with an emphasis on informal learning. Using "opportunity" in everyday life was a factor in people's self-directed efforts. There was a general sense that people found ways to convert the resources they had in order to take control of their lives and meet some of their own needs within a limited range of choice.

Relying on the help and assistance of others was evidenced in numerous accounts. Maria talked of her strategies for learning English. As a youth, she listened very carefully to Anglos she encountered at the local grocery store and other public locations. Although she did not attend school, she practiced English with her brothers and sisters who did go. As a young adult, Maria's husband read English language comic books, she made friends with Anglo farmhands, and ventured along with her husband on his trips to town. "I had new friends. I was the farmer's lady, and I used to go over there to the house parties. I made them understand [my English], and they did too. I learned how to talk English. I learned because by seeing and asking questions and everything. I do everything I want to now. I somehow, I know everything I need to know." As an older adult, her children, particularly her daughter, assist her with mail and paying bills. Maria reciprocates by teaching her grandchildren Spanish.

> We talk a lot of Spanish, and I try to talk to my grandkids in Spanish. I talk to them in Spanish, and they answer me in English, but they understand me. I want them to learn Spanish.

Other individuals reported getting assistance from friends or relatives with learning or improving their Spanish language skills. Regina said, "It's embarrassing when someone starts talking to you in Spanish, and they assume I understand everything they're saying, so I asked one of my friends to teach me." For Ana, "My mother knows more Spanish than I do, so when I visit her now we speak some Spanish so I can brush up on it."

Additional examples of informal learning are documented through reading and study projects including reading a variety of materials at home, researching one's own family history by drawing up a family tree, volunteering in a nephew's pre-school program, learning and trying out family recipes passed down through multiple generations, and investigating educational options for one's children.

Judith talked with me at a community center while she was waiting for one of the center's assistants to type up a legal letter for her regarding an unemployment claim. She had handwritten what she wanted to say in the letter, and the woman assisting her typed it up, corrected the spelling and grammar, and put it in the appropriate professional format. Judith's reliance on another person's skills to complement her own skills and knowledge affirms a community of assistance, which is a strong value in the Chicano/a community.

In addition to examples of informal learning and helping each other, individual stories document numerous examples of on-the-job training. Gloria reported she learned how to do a job she wanted at a factory at which she worked. She knew it required a college credential, but since she had neither that nor a high school diploma, she had a friend teach her everything about quality control. When she felt confident about her level of knowledge and skill and a job opening was available, she requested a transfer upgrade, which she successfully accomplished.

Eduardo reported he had welding skills but did not know how to read blueprints, so he sought opportunities to learn little by little until he reached such a level of expertise that he could market his skills. Numerous examples exist in the individual stories. In all examples, people created learning opportunities by taking advantage of the situation they found themselves in and of the resources available.

Characteristics of Resistance and Production

These are individuals of action, people who have taken it upon themselves to confront the realities of their lives and move beyond the structural and cultural constraints they have encountered. Through the creation of autonomous social spaces, they have drawn upon their own resources, limited as they may be, for assertion of dignity and pride.

The notion of cultural action with an emphasis on asserting cultural values can be very helpful in understanding the actions people engage in as they press up against limiting and oppressive structural mechanisms of society. These individuals have experienced exclusion not only in educational settings as youth, but have struggled with social, economic, cultural, and political inequities throughout their lives and the lives of their ancestors as well. The continuous, cumulative reality of one's experiences defies the compartmentalization of analysis. As people realize that they have been subordinated to an inferior status, through reflexive monitoring of social interactions and social settings, they come to realize they deserve more. The power to act and the intentional, or purposeful, character of their actions becomes a continuous flow of conduct as people demand justice. In these moments of culture, people use their power to intervene in events and to alter their course. This ability to act in pursuit of one's own interests is informed by both experience and reflection upon those experiences. Practices of resistance and production, therefore, can be understood as strategic conduct that reaffirms a commitment to sustain cultural identity.

The table, Defining Characteristics of Strategic Resistance and Production (Table 6.1), delineates the multiple strategies of resistance and production, the factors contributing to those actions, personal attributes that exemplify the action, and verbatim quotes that illustrate the personal attributes. This typology positions strategic action taken by educationally unserved Chicanos/as in the pursuit of satisfying educational needs and desires. A continuum of activities used to resist the dominant discourse of what it means to be part of the undereducated "minority" population supports a view of people as knowing actors who have the power to intervene in life events. Knowledge and reflection on that knowing, based on past and contemporary lived experiences that demean and devalue culture and identity, are used to inform subsequent actions. People have the power to intervene through strategic conduct in life events and to alter their course.

These potential responses of how people deal with their educational marginality should not be taken as exhaustive or mutually exclusive. Further, individuals employed a number of responses or strategies, either simultaneously or successively, over the course of adulthood. Each set of actions is characterized by distinct contributing factors and personal attributes. For example, acts of refusal are concerned with moral issues of justice as a response to repeated discrimination and subordination. Objections to getting less than others in society, whether economically, educationally, or socially, were voiced by those who refused involvement with traditional programs. There is a stated awareness of one's place in society and its class-based nature, which leads to a power of will that influences subsequent action.

There is an outright rejection of one's predefined place as exemplified by the statement, "Having a diploma really don't have nothing to do with it." Two dimensions are evident within the statements of rejection that illustrate this set of strategies. For some, it means a clear reliance on cultural roles. "I never needed to go back to school. My

Strategies of Resistance & Production	Contributing Factors	Attributes	Illustrations
Acts of Refusal	Moral issues Time and again The power of will	* Rejection of one's societal place * Turning one's back upon the dominant discourse	"Having a diploma really don't have nothing to do with it." "If you do a good job, it doesn't seem like it should make any difference."
Avoidance	Relations Time Issues Sympathetic affections	* Wait-&-see attitude * Steering clear of unsupportive disrespectful environments	"I know I won't go back there. It was a waste of my time.... I haven't thought about finding another program."
Alternatives	Formation of ideas Change Innovation	* Reliance on variations and substitutions * Looking for compatible options * Change of one thing for another	"I want a good job...so I've gone back a few times but I never liked the programs."
Preferences	Time appropriate Spatial order Promotion of ideas Limited choices	* Finding voice and advocating for self * Culling the options * Furthering one's interests * Setting priorities	"They have to want to spend time with people, they have to communicate more, they have to give people recognition."
Opportunites to learn	Opportunity Reciprocal assistance Ethic of care	* Drawing upon resources * Correspondence to cultural values * Self-directed projects	"My mother knows more Spanish than I do, so when I visit her now we speak some Spanish so I can brush up on it."

Table 6.1
Defining Characteristics of Strategic Resistance and Production

husband always worked and I raised our daughter." For others, it indicates a reliance on other cultural values, in this case, of integrity. "If you do a good job, it doesn't seem like it should make any difference." Thus, this strategy indicates that some individuals turn their back upon the dominant discourse as well as turning their back on one's predetermined societal place.

Strategies of avoidance concern issues of relations, time, and sympathetic affections. This type of action indicates people are avoiding relationships that are not supportive of their goals and/or relationships that may even be disrespectful and uncaring. There is a direct link between present-day situations and events of the past. Memories of feeling cheated, not respected, not assisted in educational efforts, have caused some individuals to withdraw in order to protect cultural identity and values.

Characteristic of this strategy is a wait-and-see attitude indicating hesitancy, fear, a sense of being unsure. Equally evident in the texts is a firmness of conviction, a knowing of what is safe and what is not safe, what is comfortable and what is not comfortable, as illustrated by these comments by Elena and Olivia, "I know I won't go back there. It was a waste of my time," and "nobody wanted to take the time even after all these years. So I haven't changed my mind."

Seeking alternatives as a strategy of resistance and production indicates concern with change and the formation of ideas and innovation. When people are looking for alternative educational options, they have determined they have needs that they want to satisfy. Some individuals also seem to be aware of different programs in their communities and have some ideas about what facilitates their learning. Searching for a program that meets their needs indicates both an interest in fitting into the community and a determination to find suitable ways to accomplish this goal. Another aspect that is revealed is a reliance on one's character as opposed to educational credentials.

Individuals who seek alternatives are not only looking for compatible options in terms of meeting educational needs and in creating one's place within the dominant culture. There is a qualifier; there is a desire to be treated fairly and equitably. One rendition of this attribute is, "I want a good job...so I've gone back a few times, but I never liked the programs."

Defining preferences as a strategy of resistance and production holds that by reflecting on past and contemporary experiences, individuals, through systematic assessment, come to decisions about the options that are presented to them. Factors involved in determining preferences center on issues of time, spatial order, promotion of ideas, and limited choices. The factors of time reflect situations in the past that serve as both a measure of history and expectations. Spatial order indicates there are boundaries on preferences that reflect cultural values and beliefs. Within a preferred set of options, there is acknowledgment that individuals must choose within a set of limited choices.

Personal attributes indicative of this strategy, whereby one defines preferences, include finding one's voice and advocating on one's own behalf, culling the options, furthering one's interests, and setting priorities. Characteristic of this action is "[the teachers] have to want to spend time with people, they have to communicate more, they have to give people recognition." Some individuals were very specific about their standard criteria in reference to adult education programs that could assist them in meeting their needs. A reliance on cultural values of care and community, treating people with dignity, and sharing educational knowledge and resources are a few of the criteria people use to describe programs in which they would consider enrolling.

Finally, through the creation of multiple and innovative opportunities to learn, people move beyond the rejection of the educational system to form their own self-directed and self-defined projects. Reciprocal assistance and an ethic of care, indicative of cultural values, plus time factors, help to define opportunities to learn as both a strategy of resistance and a strategy of production.

Drawing upon resources and knowledge in local communities and through networks of family and friends, individuals actively seek assistance in the pursuit of their goals whether it is learning Spanish, having another person write checks, or tracking down family history. The assistance requested is always reciprocated through gestures of mutual assistance. Those who create opportunities for learning through self-directed projects exhibit a high degree of correspondence to cultural values. This strategy relies on others within the community rather than outside agencies. Indicative of this approach is the comment by Ana, "My mother knows more Spanish than I do, so when I visit her now we speak some Spanish so I can brush up on it."

While challenging the dominant discourse that defines undereducated and unserved adults as incompetent, stupid, and outsiders, people create and utilize a range of strategies of resistance and production of meaning. These strategies, or practices, are both informed by, and influence, social experiences. Individuals counter discriminatory practices by relying on values preferred by the Chicano/a culture: values of ethical care, assistance, and understanding.

Contradictions are evident in some of the strategies employed. Although rejected by, and, subsequently rejecting, the dominant school system, it was found that a majority of the individuals have attempted to use traditional adult education programs to further their educational goals. These educational agencies have pushed people to the margins once again by their discriminatory and exclusionary practices that ensure that the status quo is maintained.

Acts of refusal reject, almost totally, dominant cultural values, yet in the end, are supportive of the mainstream by limiting available options for economic and social mobility. It is only through continual experimentation and creation of opportunities that affirm one's cultural identity, that people can oppose oppression, and thus, open the possibility of transforming reality.

Stages of resistance appear to exist. Individuals recounted youth educational experiences that indicated an internal struggle to stay in school and complete their education while at the same time experiencing continual humiliation, cultural disregard, and exclusion by teachers, administrators, and peers. After entering the labor force and realizing, once again, they are rejected by society, they recount similar personal and family/friend experiences of discrimination. Nevertheless, with a desire to somehow "fit in" to the dominant society, individuals continue to strive to integrate into the mainstream. Rather than renounce who they are in order to accommodate the system, these individuals want to retain their cultural identity. The internal struggle continues as the dominant society imposes its concept of reality. Gramsci's (1971) work insists on the power of individuals to contest the control of the dominant society and the resulting need for the dominant class to reimpose its world view since it is in constant danger of being questioned and resisted. As adults, these Chicano/a individuals indicate numerous attempts to modify their educational situations by engaging in a variety of strategies that create the means to oppose and change the status quo. Over the course of time, people appear to continue to strive for inclusion yet refuse, to varying degrees, to accommodate to the dominant culture.

Resisting practices are efforts to sustain cultural integrity and represent persistence in contesting the control of the dominant society. Not only do individuals perceive their educational needs, but they exhibit a continuing interest in learning as self-directed learners. Non-involvement in traditional adult basic education and English literacy programs should be seen as resistance to educational practices of exclusion, marginality, and cultural disregard for Chicanos/as, in particular, and may well reflect strategic actions of other nondominant groups, in general.

Chapter 7
Conflicts of
Ideology and Practice

> There are few options open to the actors in question, given that they behave rationally, rationally in this case meaning effectively aligning motives with the end-result of whatever conduct is involved. (Giddens 1984, 178)

I have provided a sociocultural lens through which to view the stories of Maria, Jose, Patricia, Carlos, Olivia, and the other Chicano/a men and women who talked with me about their learning experiences and their attempts to meet their self-identified educational needs of reading, writing, and English literacy. Learning and literacy skills are individual social activities of engagement that people undertake as part of growing and maturing, as a part of learning skills of communication and interaction. Literacy abilities are initial and foundational skills, skills that are built upon as knowledge is constructed and created; abilities that anyone who attends school is tested on over and over again bench marking progress and denoting areas of strength or weakness. It is no wonder, then, that we tend to see literacy as individual attainment or individual failure. The social nature of literacy is masked, the group aspects of learning are forgotten, the cultural and class differences absent from view. The structural mechanisms that promote some while holding others back are invisible. Underlying assumptions of this type of individualized viewpoint suggest that everyone has the same educational opportunities and access, the same resources of quality programs and top-notch teachers, along with the same everyday gender, culture, economic, social, and political experiences that define and facilitate understanding dominant patterns and ideologies of mainstream society.

As this thinking goes, individual motivation is a key determinate to success. Biased test construction is preceded by biased worldviews, and although we live in a multicultural world that more and more people accept as reality, measurement and assessment instruments continue to reflect the dominant experience-base of the white, Eurocentric middle class. Focusing on the individual and individual attainment assumes that the so-called meritocractic system of education achieves for each individual the opportunity of success through hard work. This is a myth that needs to be debunked.

By using a sociocultural lens, we can see just how social structures and cultural preferences are used to keep not only individuals in their place, but whole groups of people; people like Chicanos/as of the Southwest who are still seen by some as foreigners, deficient in English language skills and American culture. Contradictions and conflict emerge for all nondominant groups in the United States, however, from the particulars of a singular case, we can ultimately derive learning (Stake 1994, 240), learning that delineates the differences and contradictions that Chicanos/as must contend with as they press against the social structure of education and schooling. Cultural aspects of difference reflect the areas of struggle and discrimination that are likely to occur in the educational arena. Continuous discrimination and struggle are interlocking themes that permeate all aspects of life. We heard about people being tracked into low-wage, low-skill jobs; differential public services such as police protection in most Chicano/a neighborhoods; ridicule of language differences in community and work settings; and separated enclaves of Latino communities within larger cities.

Stavans (1995) asks if the American Dream is accessible only when one denies one's own past, for example for the three-fifths of

Mexican Americans "who were in these territories even before the pilgrims arrived on the Mayflower, and only unexpectedly, unwillingly became part of the United States when the Treaty of Guadalupe Hidalgo was signed. Twice American in spite of ourselves: American americanos," (197) "still traveling from marginality to acceptance in the United States" (168). The contemporary conditions witnessed and experienced by the men and women here in educational arenas, and in society in general, attest to the continuing struggles as they travel the allies of marginality and create ways to retain cultural dignity and gain necessary skills for today's society.

In furthering understanding, it might be helpful to look at the specific aspects of human agency, cultural action, and adult education structures within this particular case; how they manifest and interact; and the dialectics of agency and structure.

Efforts to Reach Educational Goals

In this study all individuals left school prior to completing requirements for a high school diploma or, in some cases, prior to achieving English literacy skills of reading and writing. All individuals indicated educational needs in specific literacy areas such as reading comprehension, spelling, pronunciation of certain words, writing skills, and math. There were also individuals who desired vocational skill training but saw their low academic skills as stumbling blocks. Included in people's testimonies were statements of desires to upgrade skills, regret at not "sticking it out," and determination to reach certain learning goals such as upgrading Spanish language abilities or learning about one's family history. They were quite clear about their academic skill abilities and were able to articulate what specific skills they wanted and why.

It is really important to comprehend how people make sense of their struggle to get an education if we are to understand their perspectives of their realities. Historically, as Mirande (1985) reminds us, "the primary function of schooling from the earliest days on has been to extinguish the culture of the Chicanos and to mute their language" (97). Stavans (1995) believes that "once again, the young people are pushed to the margins, their journey from the barrio to the classroom marked by depression....What's wrong is a lack of genuine interest by the institutions themselves" (183). We see in these comments the dual nature

of the struggle: the social and structural dimensions of socialization, oppression, ideology, power, and the individual response of internalized
blame and shame. When we turn to the comments of the men and
women, similar connections can be made. Recall Julia's multiple reasons for leaving school at the age of seventeen. She related a series of
circumstances that were present including family poverty and her need
to get a job and help out financially. This was an acceptable reason for
leaving school; another dimension of her situation that was even more
troublesome from her perspective was the lack of safety she experienced each day at school. As I talked with her further, she told me she
could not get the teachers to believe her about the problems she was
having with the African American girl gang that consistently threatened her. Julia reached out to the teachers for help and safety, yet they
turned away from her. She was told to deal with it. How is one to learn,
to engage in learning, when safety is an issue and when teachers turn
the other way. Do we call this favoritism, racism, or simply neglect?
Bertha named her struggle with trying to get an education as one of
favoritism.

> They didn't care if I finished work in school. They had their
> favorites they worked with. I needed more one-on-one, but I
> couldn't get it.

Favoritism was also evident in Sandra's story of the cultural preferences of the school when she wore the Chicano colors on her clothing.
The principal told her she could not wear ethnic colors to school, it
might cause trouble. The principal's attempt to mute Sandra's cultural
pride violated her freedom of individual expression. This act sent multiple messages such as "be silent," "be the same as others," "difference
can cause dissent," "don't call attention to yourself but blend in with
the mainstream," and "there is no tolerance or value for difference."
These messages were not only for Sandra but other Chicano/a students
as well. The predominance of mainstream fashions that students wore
apparently was not considered a problem by administration or uncomfortable for students who did not identify with the dominant culture.

We cannot overlook the economic differentials of the barrio, or in-
ner city, neighborhood schools. The persistence of gangs and intimida-
tion that stifle students, the adult education programs that require
traveling long distances on public transportation to unsafe neighborhoods, often in inadequately lit industrial locations, and the

disorganization of teachers who seem to be unprepared, according to those who have participated in such programs, highlight the depressed environment and lack of resources found there. Adult basic education and English literacy programs rely heavily on volunteers who have no previous teaching experience with adults or, in some cases, no previous teaching experience at all. Strapped with low costs per pupil that are touted as a cost saving to taxpayers, adult basic education programs themselves struggle at the bottom of the educational hierarchy.

Recall also the numerous stories of those who turned to alternative schools after either leaving or being pushed out of home high schools. The alternative schools supposedly offer another option for those who have trouble conforming to mainstream school standards but, in fact, these alternative schools relied on the same ideology of conformism and difference as deficient as the mainstream schools. And recall Olivia's words, "We were always the outsiders." As adults, the struggle continues as some people search for ways to upgrade their skills. Patricia uses her husband's old textbooks; Maria seeks help and assistance from family, friends, and even strangers so that she can take care of her financial and business obligations. Maria told me she would have liked school if she had the opportunity to attend but the economic and cultural constraints of her life limited her education and schooling.

Carlos, Norma, and Jose explain their struggle to get an education by economic standards, in reference to their work, and the lack of connection between education and work. They believe that a diploma would not make a difference in the kinds of jobs they can get. They understand that the credential that is touted as the entry ticket would not have helped them get more than manual labor, low wage, positions; these are the fields they see open to them whether they have that piece of paper or not. Unfortunately, recognizing the structural reasons for the struggle does not necessarily lead to solutions that ameliorate the situation. Bertha, Olivia, Sandra, Eduardo, and others would feel better about themselves if they had been able to complete school. As Gloria stated, "It was my fault. I didn't have the guts to stick it out," while Patricia told me she had not considered how much of a struggle it had been for her to get an education prior to us talking about it. Even as an adult, Olivia recounts one episode after another of finding similar conditions in different types of adult education programs all resulting in diminishing her self-esteem and her ability to learn. The paradox, of course, is that while some people can see the structural and cultural barriers placed in their way, they revert to blaming themselves and internalizing failure as they feel powerless to change the system. Some people think if they had done something differently, the outcome might have been different.

The historical significance of oppression from the early days of colonization remains part of people's social and cultural identity. Concealing history functions as a central strategy of an oppressive colonial discourse (Macedo and Bartolome 2000), yet the political, economic, and ideological nature of the colonization process provokes a reaction from the people who are colonized. The struggle people engage in is the same struggle of their ancestors, family members, and the younger generation coming up behind them. This identity of difference and displacement (Elenes 1997) is similar to the African American identity born of struggle that Hill Collins (1990) talks about; an ancestral history of oppression that continues to embed itself in the lives of African Americans. As learners, Chicano/a adults have shared similar educational experiences in the form of discrimination, struggle, and difference. Yet, the contexts of particular educational experiences varied greatly among them, across time and space, each one attaining different levels of education and English literacy skills. Through individual and group oppression and subordination, one comes to know a way of being that is outside the mainstream. This knowing is informed by experience and grounded in the real world.

For people engaged in the struggle of learning the ways and language of the dominant culture, while trying to retain their historical ethnic identity, it is an ambiguous struggle. There are benefits to knowing the dominant language and culture, and people are required to learn it in order to survive, yet, at the same time, there is always the risk of losing a sense of the ethnic self. Chicanos/as would be foolish to remain totally outside the English language. Language assimilation, however, strips people of their indigenous community, a result of the ideological nature of colonization. Regrettably for some, there has been little room for compromise or negotiation which could blend multiple ideologies of identity and culture. A series of counteractions against colonization seems inevitable and stretches across generations as the colonization process continues. Feeling guilt, shame, and regret for forfeiting one's language, people reclaimed their language, their voice, and their identity; they used their subjective knowledge to regain their power. There is a strong preference for integrating one's self and the group into society where cultural identity and difference are allowed, rather than acculturating to values that are contrary to Chicano/a values.

While their struggle to get an education is informed by experiences of exclusion, however, these individuals are not simply victims but knowledgeable actors who are making their own history. People who reject the dominant discourse act as knowing subjects. The subsequent actions they engage in are utilized to fight oppression. As adults, their perceptions and the decisions they make regarding further actions to meet educational needs are influenced by these past experiences as well as by their own responses to their everyday realities.

The Politics of Cultural Actions

Clearly, it is difficult to get an education if you are a Mexican American in Colorado or the Southwest. As individuals interact with the dominant culture, they expect a fair shake and the opportunity to contribute to the larger society. Finding opportunities closed to them, they struggle with an internal conflict between the need to sustain and affirm cultural identity and the desire to get an education. Their educational experiences as youth begin to formulate this double bind for people. As adults, they continue to struggle with the same issues whereby they strive to meet self-identified educational needs only to find situational environments reaffirming their marginal status rather than affirming their group ethos and cultural identity.

It is in adult life that individuals must confront the limited options open to them; they continue to witness, and personally experience, exclusion at every turn. They have tried to fit into mainstream society on their own terms but are continually rejected. For some people, this consciousness results in a demand for social justice; individual or group actions of resistance and production are instigated with widely varying outcomes. Using the resources they have, individuals take what control they can of their lives in order to challenge and counter their marginal status.

Whether challenging the dominant discourse of conformity and necessary subordination into mainstream culture that assaults at every

turn, or pulling back in order to advance later, individuals engage in actions that reaffirm and sustain cultural identity as they pursue their perceived educational needs. People know a great deal about the conditions of social reproduction and the systems of inequalities of the
society in which they are a member, as well as their place within that society. This knowing is considered to be "practical consciousness," or
tacit knowledge, which results from the reflexive monitoring of social
settings and interactions. Subsequent actions, or strategic conduct
then, supports the interests of the individual and/or the group. Incorpo-
rating such values as cooperation, mutual history and understanding,
and respect, everyday practices reflect attempts to challenge and transform a troubling reality. At a discursive level, people can often talk
about their actions and the reasons for those actions, exhibiting intentionality of purpose. "Resistance starts by using received knowledges to
ask critical questions about the nature of the social order. Resistance
also means seeing small acts as cumulative and significant for social
change. Resistance must also eschew pragmatism and recognize the
limits of agency" (Dei 2000, 39). It is not implausible to suppose that
those in subordinate positions, in fact, might have a greater penetra-
tion, or understanding, of the conditions of social reproduction than
those who dominate them (Giddens 1979). This greater understanding
of the unequal structures in society enables individuals in subordinated
positions to more consciously act on their own behalf. Reflecting on
past experiences and the knowledge constructed from situations of differential access and reward, people pursued actions supportive of their
own interests in learning, their own desires to complete their education, or their willingness to get the necessary skills to do their jobs or
find work. Nevertheless, in the end, the struggle continues because of
the unequal power relations inherent between the colonizers and the
colonized. The struggle cannot be won, once and for all. Rather, the dialectical relationship between the individual and society signifies a continuous struggle that is in a constant state of flux and movement. The
hegemonic nature of the dominant power is not reified and always
holds the possibility of change and transformation, albeit it can never
be an easy or swift transformation.

What are the consequences of the strategic actions of resistance
and production people have taken so far in their lives? Cecilia's closing
comments to me suggest that some people have come to know their

own sense of agency. When I asked her what opportunities or limitations she saw for herself, she told me the following:

> What I've been through has given me an open mind. I didn't really make the choices. I kinda got pushed into one thing and another, and then I took the opportunity to direct my life.

Cecilia has gained a sense of the way things are in the real world and the effort she must put forth in order to create some opportunities for herself. Cecilia was a welfare mother for a short time after she got hurt on the job, but when I met her, she already had a long history of working, first as a janitor and housekeeper in a cleaning business that she helped to build, then for a bonding and processing service that she helped get organized. She went to an alternative school for her junior year of high school but left shortly after to get married; her husband left about a year after their daughter was born. On welfare, Cecilia was directed to a GED preparation program, but left that program as well. She told me, "The students weren't serious and the teachers didn't settle them down." She felt it was a waste of her time when she needed to find work. At another point, she attended a local community center for a few months, where she again studied for the GED tests but left before taking all of the required tests because of long work hours. Keeping herself employed and providing for her family were her priorities, and they came before completing her formal education. Cecilia's search for alternatives that fit her lifestyle as a strategy for getting an education has not gotten Cecilia a GED certificate, but it has given her the knowledge that she can make choices, it has provided her with information about various options, and it has helped her gain knowledge about what is important to her. Her struggle to get an education and the strategy of looking for alternatives also seems to have prepared her for monitoring the education of her children who she removed from the public school where there was too much violence and not enough attention given to students. She had them enrolled in a private Catholic school that met her criteria of a good school.

The structures of society and its mechanisms often constrain the needs, desires, and actions of some people, while enabling those of others. Traditional adult basic educational programs, for example, advance the racist interests of the dominant society and do not promote diverse cultural values. While social structures are uneven between individuals and/or groups, structural dimensions of society also have both constraining and enabling aspects for any one individual or group. For example, the practices of adult education include control mechanisms in relation to the access of knowledge through underfunded programs and inexperienced teachers. As individuals in this study strain to deal with uncaring and racist teachers, or low-quality programs, or crowded classrooms, their frustration and demand for justice and equality, in turn, enable some of them to act on their own behalf rather than simply acquiesce to the status quo of differential access. Thus, the constraining nature of social structures and mechanisms may, in fact, facilitate action directed at furthering one's own interests. The actions taken by people illuminate this concept in that the exclusionary practices and ideology of educational systems prompt instances of resistance and production.

Whether or not having a high school diploma or GED certificate would have helped people's self-esteem or helped them feel better about themselves, being a part of the mainstream culture was clearly the most important thing to some individuals, particularly when they were teenagers. It signifies completion and success in the social mores of society—fitting in—and the subsequent key to future employment and well being. While formal schooling still conjures up negative memories for many people, it has not curtailed the hunger for knowledge and learning. Nevertheless, society ranks people according to their level of education and skill attainment, seldom taking the time to understand the social, political, and cultural context of people's lives which accounts for lived experiences. Lack of a diploma or certificate is seen by the general public as lack of commitment or interest in learning.

In each case, we can examine what resources people have gained or lost depending on their choices of action. While some have advanced either in their job, family, or community, each has done so with the help of others in their communities. Just as challenges for equal schooling have been a part of Chicano/a politics since the 1960s, people continue to engage in alternative group action, maintaining both a political core and cultural communities as they fight for their rights to educational access. Further, Chicanos/as counter the unequal power relations by intentional engagement in the ongoing struggle. They do this by joining with family members to recover lost histories, by assisting

Spanish-speaking individuals with English translation when needed, by opening businesses in Chicano neighborhoods, by frequenting local ethnic community centers and businesses, by attending festivals and other cultural events that strengthen solidarity and group identity, and by taking the manual labor jobs or whatever it takes to support and maintain families.

Sociocultural Conflicts Limiting Participation

The differential power relations between Mexican American culture and the dominant society, and the subsequent struggles to get an education, signal the need to take a closer look at some of the specific conflicts that underlie these struggles. Three types of sociocultural conflicts limit the participation of Chicanos/as in traditional adult basic education and English literacy programs. These include conflicts over the various purposes of adult basic education and English literacy; conflicts due to diverse cultural identities among adult students, teachers, and administrators; and conflicting cultural ideologies which dictate what is of value and the how of expressing oneself. These conflicts often foster educational discrimination and subordination in adult programs. As a consequence, the men and women here have decided that formalized programs are not for them.

Purposes of Adult Basic Education and English Literacy

Basic academic skills of reading, writing, thinking, and speaking, or adult literacy, are forms of constructing meaning within a sociocultural context. People use basic skills of literacy to communicate within their cultural worlds; literacy is also a product of cultural activity. Such an understanding helps us think about the educational purposes, adult learners, and localized contexts in which skill development, literacy, and learning occurs. While adult basic education espouses opportunities for learning, promising increased capacity and skill development, it often does so in a decontextualized way, ignoring the language, lives, and lived experiences of the adults who enroll in programs. Rather, basic skills are taught as if everyone, including the diverse teachers, administrators, and students, uses language and literacy skills for the same purposes and in the same ways. Instruction is constructed for

middle-class, Anglo lives, in ways that create conflicting demands between the two cultures for Mexican Americans. In other words, adult
basic education and English literacy limit access to what people can
learn, set variable conditions under which learning occurs, and has
standardized and institutionalized mechanisms for social control and
hegemonic purposes. The standardization of instruction and management of the classroom purposely ignores the diversity within the learning environment and the larger social community. Teachers as agents
of the state promote the status quo of the dominant culture; Chica-
nos/as as agents attempt to meet their cultural needs within a system
that strives to assimilate them and deny their culture and language. In-
variably teachers, learners, and the system collide under such
conditions.

Distinguishing the difference between individual teachers who are
not interested or not prepared to work with Chicano/a adults, and the
hegemonic role of the teacher as agent of the state in the classroom to
model, train, and monitor socialization into the dominant culture,
helps us to understand how social systems work. Instructors are expected to utilize the dominant teaching materials, methods, and techniques that guide adult basic education practice, they are expected to
have an interest in assisting people in learning basic academic skills
which will help them move around in the world more easily and effectively, but it is a standardized world that is seen, one that conforms to a
normative local community, society, and nation. This is not to say that
individual teachers should not be held accountable for their actions
and attitudes or that retraining teachers is futile. Rather, it suggests the
hegemonic nature of all aspects of schooling and the intensity of the restructuring job ahead.

People use literacy to achieve their goals in a variety of contexts.
There is a need to understand that people have their own purposes for
adult basic education and they move through programs in their own
ways. Their goals may be different from, or even conflict with, the purposes of educational programs; their lack of interest in moving along a
developmental track can be reason enough to leave a program that is
considered inadequate to their purposes. Adults are always looking for
something in particular when they enroll in an educational program,
something that will advance their ability to interact in a contextualized
and cultural world. It is this intentionality and goal setting of adult

learning, and their unmet expectations, that suggest ineffective mechanisms and practices. Inadequate settings where unskilled teachers, low quality or disorganized programs, teacher-centered prescribed curricula, or ineffective classroom environments contribute to marginalization and isolation. This idea is reinforced by the double bind situation whereby individuals look to the educational institution to further their economic, social, and cultural needs, yet must reject particular settings because of discrimination, subordination, and lack of caring.

With a predominant purpose of socializing adult learners into mainstream culture, the lack of intercultural understanding and respect on the part of adult basic education teachers remind Mexican Americans of similar experiences in the realms of their social, political, and economic lives where they are constructed as cultural "Others." The monolingual, monocultural educational settings supported by middle-class, Anglo instructors requires that learners forget who they are and strive for the dominant culture espoused in adult programs.

How is it that there is so little intercultural understanding and respect? It is quite ironic to consider adult basic education and English literacy programs as showing a lack of intercultural understanding when, in fact, the majority of students in these programs represent not only numerous cultures, races, and ethnic groups, but various class groups as well. Historically, these programs were developed and designed as a way to process individuals into the true American citizens, the socialization process was an Americanizing one where diverse individuals and their cultures would be homogenized to look the same. While there are conflicting modes of discourse about the purposes of schooling in the United States, the socializing role, dominant in elementary and secondary schooling, is still a predominate feature of adult basic education. As a result, there is limited interest in advancing or preserving other cultures, ethnic or otherwise.

Diverse Cultural Identities

Everyone has a cultural identity, in fact, multiple identities. This fact seems to elude many people in the dominant United States culture as they move from one cultural group to another in the course of their daily lives. For those who prefer to ignore this notion, it is white, Eurocentric privilege that allows them the luxury of doing so. Nevertheless, as society struggles with the multiple and hugely diverse groups that call the United States home, cultural identity is an anchor for many people that links them to others and a preferred way of being.

I was told in multiple ways over and over again by the Mexican Americans that "my language is my identity." So I see the struggle over language as especially representative of the ongoing conflict of not only shifting Chicano/a identities (Flores and Yudice 1990), but the subsequent conflict among diverse adult students, teachers, and administrators. One of the important keys to understanding the language as identity phenomena is the ideological nature of language. Language penetrates its ideology (Freire 1985) through processes of thinking and constructing contextual knowledge of concrete reality. It creates habits of being and doing in the world, building and shaping culture, shaping knowledge of the world, and expressions of that knowledge. According to Freire there is "the dominant need to inculcate in the dominated a negative attitude toward their own culture. The former encourage the latter to reject their own culture by instilling a false comprehension of their culture as something ugly and inferior,...furthermore, the dominant impose their way of being, talking" (192). There is a general sense of loss regarding the Spanish language. Forced to assimilate into the dominant culture by accommodating to different cultural values and language, Chicanos/as experience this loss as regret, shame, and conflict. For most, the accommodation has not paid off, and there is a growing movement to relearn or reintegrate Spanish into public life.

"The experiences of uniting, of speaking a different and forbidden speech, of discovering that this speech is valid (though forbidden), of seeing that this speech is beautiful (even though some say it is ugly): these experiences are cultural and belong to the culture of dominated people. The more dominated people mobilize within their culture, the more they unite, grow, and dream" (Freire, 1985, 192). Openly using one's language increases pride in who one is. It becomes a way of reaffirming a positive sense of self and group identity. Language difference is viewed by the dominant culture as deviance from cultural, linguistic, social, and political norms. Adult education, as part of the public education system, extends this ideological stance by requiring Chicanos/as to leave their Spanish at the door, thus controlling resources through local politics and relying on English-only laws.

Chicanos/as must continually move back and forth across cultural borders as they interface with the contemporary power structures of mainstream society. As they traverse the boundaries into the public sphere of daily experiences, "reflexively monitoring" (Giddens 1979, 6) behavior and the setting, a process of strategic negotiation takes place as a result of discontinuities, contradictions, and oppositions, rather than as a result of the continuities and coincidence between themselves and the social contexts of everyday life. The continuous movement between two cultural worlds requires that they become adept at shifting consciousness "from one group's perception of social reality to another, and at times to perceive multiple social realities without losing their sense of self-coherence" (Hurtado 1996, 384). The knowledge obtained through shifting consciousness is more political and structural than rational or intuitive. The ability to shift consciousness as one moves back and forth across cultural borders also causes Chicanos/as to have multiple voices in order to talk to different audiences without losing a sense of coherence. The structure of social life in communities allows Chicanos/as to withdraw to smaller, and often safer, private cultural networks to regroup and regain balance before once again having to interact with mainstream public communities that may be hostile.

Resistance and acts of production create autonomous spaces for both the reaffirmation of dignity and the creation of educational opportunities, while distancing one from the inaccessible mainstream society. Freire's (1985) conceptualization of resistance as a determination to free oneself, places strategic actions within a framework of meaning constructed and reconstructed to reaffirm and sustain cultural identity. Each individual's resistance is unique to his or her perceptions of his or her own personal experiences, "situational and contextual variations exist depending on the intensities of oppression" (Dei 2000, 13).

Cultural identity and the group ethos are not unidirectional. They are not only influenced and created by socially constructed experiences, but also influence and create knowledge and everyday decision making as it relates to social interactions. How the past and present intersect in people's lives frames the conditions and processes involved in constructing knowledge. Flores and Yudice (1990) talk of Latino self-formation that confronts the prevailing ethos by congregating an ethos of its own, not necessarily an outright adversarial ethos, but certainly an alternative ethos. "The Latino border transcreates the impinging dominant cultures by constituting the space for their free in-termingling—free because it is dependent on neither, nor on the reac-tion of one to the other, for its own legitimation" (74). Counter and al-ternative knowledges are flourishing (Dei 2000) as the universal claim to neutrality is questioned. The multiple lived experiences and alterna-tive knowledges "transcreated" are validated through the continual crossing of borders, thus encouraging continual development.

Differential Ideologies

It is quite clear the dominant culture is in direct conflict with the Chicano/a ethos of assistance and community, and examples abound in all aspects of life. As evidenced, there is a fundamental conflict over cultural values: individualism versus group identity, competition versus cooperation, autonomy versus community of assistance, self interests versus group interests, and isolation versus ethic of care. People related numerous educational, economic, political, cultural, and social interac-tions that reflected these conflicting ideologies. Conflicts also involved differences in how people desire to be treated. A standard of cultural re-gard that dignifies difference rather than devalues difference is clearly the preference. Additional conflicts exist in individual unwillingness to assimilate into the mainstream if that means having to give up, or sacri-fice, one's cultural identity. If the dominant society would allow en-trance, however, there are still conditions, certain standards, which people would seek. In the end, people reject the dominant culture be-cause it does not allow equal status nor does it respect diverse cultures. There is a "conditional" move towards accommodation. Nonetheless, when conditions vary too widely from the people's standards, there is reciprocal rejection of the dominant culture.

There are two dimensions to this concept of "conditional accom-modation." First, to varying degrees, people resent being relegated to predetermined positions in society based on race and resent being regu-lated through social structures such as education. Further, they reject the dominant discourse of what it means to be undereducated and dis-tance themselves from the subsequent devalued status of being under-educated through the use of discursive and nondiscursive practices, such as, claiming an attitude of not caring about educational creden-tials or ignoring dominant culture labels of themselves as unmotivated.

At a discursive level, some individuals are skeptical of the "official" view of the link between education and economics, while others make explicit the differentials to inequalities they witness and experience. Discursive practices that serve to distance also include attributing undesirable characteristics to individuals of the dominant culture, as well as grumbling, gossip, and rumor, or, what Scott (1990) calls, voices of political disguise "veiled for safety's sake" (137). Second, in a more general sense, individuals distance themselves from the dominant culture because the payoff is not worth the sacrifice. Sacrificing one's native language and the subsequent loss of identity and culture, or working hard to enter the labor market only to find limited options and low pay insufficient to care for one's family, are tests that people have used to determine the risks of assimilation. When confronting a partially closed, localized culture, individuals "distance" themselves from it as a form of "defense against the influence of outside forces that cannot otherwise easily be coped with" (Giddens 1979, 72). Not willing to give up their own histories and culture, they create parallel societies.

Individual competition, achievement, and getting ahead of others is promoted in adult basic education through teacher expectations and attitudes. This value contrasts with the Chicano/a ideology that values group as well as individual advancement, discouraging one person from advancing too far ahead of his or her family or peers. As Angelina put it:

> We like to learn all together, in a group, then we learn for the group. We have people helping each other with the language.

In a community of assistance, people share their resources to contribute to the advancement of the group, not to learn new skills in isolation. Support given today will be reciprocated in the future and everybody wins, everyone is encouraged to flourish. The Chicano/a ethos of assistance is framed within an interdependence of community. The community is only as strong as those who make up the community so it is imperative that the links that tie people together are strong. Fragmentation will eventually create isolation and the breakup of community, meaning loss of values, culture, and social identity not only for individuals but for the group as well.

The individualized self-paced instruction which values the autonomous individual denies Chicano/a learners the opportunity to work together in cooperative learning and resource sharing which is so valued in their culture. Those who experienced individualized instruction concluded they were being neglected, isolated from others and required to work alone, and thus became invisible to ongoing teacher assistance. In some cases, individuals felt they had not been identified by teachers as someone with whom it was worthwhile to work. This marginalization included a sense of anger and justified indignation, pointing to the need for culturally relevant instructional models. The hegemonic effect of adult basic education ideology is extremely powerful and will take a huge and concerted effort to transform. This is not to say that it cannot be done.

Another dimension of the ideological contrast is the patriarchal attitude of adult basic education, which assumes a greater understanding of what is best for the learner (Pai 1990). Rather than soliciting input and preferences from learners who manage adult lives filled with multiple responsibilities, adult basic education operates within the mindset of expert authority and fiscal accountability. Damage results because the implicit expectations of each cultural group limit and restrict access to meaningful cross-cultural interactions and possible transformation.

One of Olivia's reasons for lack of interest in adult basic education is that she "would have to go all the way back" and complete work for the GED test and credentials rather than working on specific sets of skills she has identified as her daily needs. Adult basic education, in an effort to standardize programs for purposes of funding accountability, has adopted a linear developmental approach to adult learning that has nothing to do with expressed desires and needs of learners and everything to do with following a prescribed ladder of credentialing. Two notions of cultural conflict can be noted here. First, a developmental approach to learning signifies a model or process by which cognition and learning occurs but does not question the cultural underpinnings of such a developmental model. Second, a prescribed step-wise instructional process that leads to GED certification is assumed to be the goal and the required outcome of all adult learners who look to upgrade basic academic skills. It does not take into account the sociocultural context of literacy use nor honor the self-identified goals of competent adults.

Ethnic values of relatedness, sharing, cooperation, and community are reaffirmed by voiced concerns about programs that do not support these values. The sociocultural dynamics involved thus constrain advancement. People do not reject education or the knowledge that they could gain, they reject programs that do not meet their educational needs, or sustain their cultural identities. Individuals view their culture as active, as dynamic, and rooted in traditions that are evolving and sustaining. Chicano/as use their subjective knowledge to regain their power and recreate their place in the larger society.

Theory to Practice

The exclusionary practices documented here have dramatic implications for the practice of adult basic education and English literacy that cannot be ignored. I have used the language of culture and difference, subordination and oppression to reveal racist hegemonic structures and sociocultural factors that play out not only in everyday life but in the practice of adult basic education and English literacy. Whether it is this language or the language of antiracist education or critical multiculturalism, there is a need to take what we know and put it into practice. I agree with Nieto (1998) who says that it is really not a lack of data but a lack of will and resources to transform discriminatory schooling practices that is the problem. By purposefully showcasing the stories of those who have direct experience with oppressive social and educational conditions there is the chance that oppositional and counter knowledges can be both solidified and used to transform education.

All the individuals in this study are interested in learning and advancing their academic skill levels, are deeply embedded and connected to their culture, and have attempted to reach their educational goals in unique ways. As eligible, but nonparticipating adults, these individuals are self-directed learners searching for solutions. The following statements can be made:

- Citing discriminating past elementary and secondary school experiences as reasons that people do not enroll in mainstream adult basic education programs masks the discriminatory practices of adult basic education and the choices people make based on those adult experiences. Not only do people experience discrimination in early experiences of schooling but in adult education programs as well. Remember that "word of mouth works both ways" (Reuben) and people tell each other about bad programs and which programs to avoid. As a result of talking with individuals who are not currently participating in adult programs due to lack of teacher sensitivity, lack of intercultural understanding, and lack of quality programs, a fuller awareness of the factors that influence nonparticipation can be attained. Further, by listening to the perceptions of these individuals, faulty adult basic education and English literacy practices that are unconscious and unintended, for example, isolated individualized instruction can be discovered and, subsequently, can be changed.

- Notions of adult basic education as a "second chance program" for adults who have failed to make it through still flourish. This popular idea conceals the tight link between K-12 education and adult education as one system organized around purposes of socialization, American mainstream values, and accountability. What in fact we guarantee when invoking the second chance rhetoric is a second chance for adults to socially reproduce into their allocated space within society. Thus, they are given another chance to fit in, assimilate, and conform to middle-class Eurocentric standards and worldviews.

- Notions of voluntary attendance and "dropout" in adult basic education and English literacy give the appearance that people do not want to participate in programs or they do not see any personal need for skill improvement while ignoring the structural problems and the ideology that guides and maintains them. Clearly, the individuals are interested in further and continual learning as evidenced by their efforts and strategies for meeting their educational needs and desires. Adults are always learning whether through life roles and responsibilities or personal desire or curiosity. When society, as well as practitioners, focuses on the failings of individuals rather than the inadequate practices of adult basic education programs, maintenance of the status quo is ensured.

- A critical multidisciplinary, multicultural approach to educational research with full participation by all racial, ethnic, gender, and class groups is required to fully expand the partial knowledge we now have regarding participation, as well as other issues, in adult basic education and English literacy. Because people's everyday reality is socially constructed around categories of race, class, and gender, people live different lives and have different frames of reference in relation to the dominant society that influence their engagement in social institutions. In order to more fully understand the everyday realities of different groups, the partial knowledge that currently exists must be expanded. Only by going directly to the individuals whom we hope to understand can we truly know how people have organized the world and the meanings they attach to what goes on in the world.

Moving more purposefully from theory to practice requires specific strategies and one of the most important is reconceptualizing the hegemonic role of the teacher (Sparks 1998). As an agent of the state, teachers are expected to morally and economically socialize individuals into the dominant culture. It is no different in adult basic education. This happens in a very definite way through the discourse of adult basic education practice.

> The discourse used in ABE [adult basic education] with its complex terms and operating assumptions constructs knowledge that defines the boundaries of practice. By looking at the discursive formations and practices...we uncover not only how practice is constructed but also the power relations inherent in these social arrangements. Dominant discourses have the power to constitute subjects and create social identities by a process of what Gee, Hull, and Lankshear (1996) call "learning inside the procedures," which ensures that practitioners take on the perspectives, the worldview, of the dominant discourse. By accepting a set of core values the practitioner masters an identity (social position) with little if any critical awareness of how that identity is constructed. Discourse thus creates, or "positions" people who, overtly or tacitly, define themselves as different, often better than others, by constructing binary relationships such as insider/outsider, literate/illiterate [teacher/student]. (Sparks and Peterson 2000, 266-267)

More time must be spent on critiquing the teacher's role as social agent thus moving away from personal attacks on individual instructors, and investigating how the role of the teacher might actually support the genuine needs of the students. By interrogating the hegemonic role of the teacher, we make visible how discriminatory practice continues to occur. An ideology of difference as deficit, which fosters teacher-directed programs, must be eliminated in order to give way to learner-centered programs. Innovative delivery of curriculum content that meshes with learners' cultural needs, interests, and desires must be rewarded. The teacher must become an advocate for all learners not just an instructor of knowledge.

From there we must look to individual practices of discrimination and ask those teachers who engage in discriminatory practices to leave or change their attitudes. Changing attitudes and views regarding low-literate adults is the first step. A genuinely antiracist perspective must be developed in order for practitioners to attain academic and social competence. Following that, teachers must teach critically about difference, exposing all learners to interactive and cooperative learning strategies. All learners need to be taught to think critically in order to question the status quo. Teacher in-service opportunities for implementing antiracist, critical multicultural adult programs using culturally relevant pedagogical materials and techniques are also needed.

Another concrete action that needs to occur requires evaluation of adult education programs for discriminatory practices that limit equitable access, quality, and respect for all learners. This might be accomplished through action research whereby teachers and administrators engage, along with learners, in investigating micropractices such as intake procedures, placement techniques, particular instructional strategies and materials, classroom climate, knowledge acquisition, and student involvement. Interventions are then designed based on what is found in local settings. These interventions are implemented and evaluated for modification. Programs and practices must relate to the needs of the target audience as defined by them, in collaboration with the instructors and administrators who offer services. This recursive process connects practitioners with learners as partners in developing nondiscriminatory programs and practices. Evaluation of programs to root out discriminatory practices means that learning environments that foster high quality, culturally relevant education, can also then be developed. Creation of critical multicultural and antiracist learner-centered systems of program delivery where

- the focus is education with the learners and builds on cultural knowledge students bring with them to the learning environment,
- learners set their own goals,

- learners collaboratively determine how their inquiry will be structured and conducted,
- multicultural perspectives are integrated into every subject area of the curriculum, and
- learners determine how they will assess their learning

will create what Dei (2000) calls a new hegemonic practice that resists oppressive social structures. A more sophisticated approach to curriculum and knowledge production takes into account the connection between social cultural identity and how knowledge is constructed.

An important aspect that does not get much attention in adult basic education and English literacy practice is the critical need to recruit Chicano/a and other culturally diverse teachers and administrators. Active recruitment, along with training and ongoing professional development for teachers of color, must replace the over reliance on middle-class whites so that culturally specific values and ideologies are predominant. The emphasis should not be on just getting teachers of color into the classrooms, however. There is, perhaps, an even greater need for administrators of color to form policies, to advocate for equal access, and to provide leadership in developing antiracist, critical multicultural programs.

There is also a need for further research and critique of adult basic education and English literacy from the perspectives of nondominant groups. Chicanos/as have a specific history of oppression, and therefore, a specific set of educational experiences, that while subordinated to the mainstream in similar ways as African Americans or Native Americans or welfare mothers, each group has different stories to tell based on their unique historical formations. These different stories tell of not just various forms of oppression but tell us what people need as they go about creating their social, cultural, economic, and political worlds. The information gained must then be taken seriously to inform practice and transformation, not just read and put onto the shelf for safe keeping. There must be a commitment to join in solidarity with our learners if social justice is to have any weight.

As this study indicates, there is substantial variability in the circumstances of individual lives, yet there is also a universal interest in furthering one's education. Adult basic education practices maintain the status quo, and a vast majority of those who live outside the dominant culture will continue to leave programs that do not attempt to help them achieve social transformation through education. While the rhetoric of inclusive educational practices is in vogue, it does not suggest the deep structural changes that are required. Our interpretation must include multiple actions directed toward change through critique of mainstream hegemonic ideologies and structures and through strategies that systematically disrupt institutions. Simply adding new cultures, bringing in additional ethnicities, or widening the circle for learners of color means that the dominant structure will remain intact. This will not do.

Bibliography

Aguayo, J. 1998. Los betabeleros (The beetworkers). In *La-gente: Hispanio history and life in Colorado,* edited by V.C. DeBaca. Denver: Colorado Historical Society.

Albert, J., and D'Amico-Samuels, D. 1991. *Adult learners' perceptions of literacy programs and the impact of participation on their lives: Phase II of a longitudinal study.* New York: Literacy Assistance Center.

Anzaldua, G. 1987. *Borderlands/La Frontera: The new mestiza.* San Francisco: Aunt Lute Books.

Baker, R. 1995. *Los dos mundos: Rural Mexican America, another America.* Logan: Utah State University Press.

———. 1996. Sociological field research with junior high school teachers: The discounting of Mexican American students. *The Journal of Educational Issues of Language Minority Students* 18 (winter): 49-66.

Barrera, M. 1979. *Race and class in the Southwest.* Notre Dame, Ind.: University of Notre Dame Press.

Beder, H. 1990. Reasons for nonparticipation in adult basic education. *Adult Education Quarterly* 40(4): 207-218.

Berg, B. 1989. *Qualitative research methods for the social sciences.* Needham Heights, Mass.: Allyn & Bacon.

Boggs, C. 1976. *Gramsci's Marxism.* London: Pluto Press.

Carmack, N. 1992. Women and illiteracy: The need for gender specific programming in literacy education. *Adult Basic Education* 2(3): 176-194.

Cervero, R., and Fitzpatrick, T. 1990. The enduring effects of family role and schooling on participation in adult education. *American Journal of Education* 99(1): 77-94.

Chavez, L. 1991. *Out of the barrio: Toward a new politics of Hispanic assimilation.* New York: Basic Books.

Clifford, J. 1986. *Writing cultures: The poetics and politics of ethnography.* Berkeley: University of California Press.

Collins, M. 1995. Critical commentaries on the role of the adult educator: From self-directed learning to postmodern sensibilities. In *In Defense of the Life World: Critical Perspectives on Adult Learning,* edited by Michael Welton. New York: State University of New York Press.

Cross, K. P. 1981. *Adults as learners: Increasing participation and facilitating learning.* San Francisco: Jossey-Bass.

Cumming, A. 1992. *Access to literacy education for language minority adults.* Washington, D.C.: Center for Applied Linguistics, ERIC Document Reproduction Service No. EDO-LE-92-02.

Cummins, J. 1994. From coercive to collaborative relations of power in the teaching of literacy. In *Literacy across language and culture,* edited by B. Federman, R. Weber, and A. Rameriz. New York: State University of New York Press.

Darkenwald, G., and Merriam, S. 1982. *Adult education: Foundations to practice.* New York: Harper & Row.

Darkenwald, G., and Valentine, T. 1985. Factor structure of deterrents to public participation in adult education. *Adult Education Quarterly* 35(4): 177-189.

De Baca, V. C. 1998. Introduction. In *La gente: Hispano history and life in Colorado,* edited by V. C. De Baca. Denver: Colorado Historical Society.

Dei, G. 2000. Towards an anti-racist discursive framework. In *Power, knowledge and anti-racism education: A critical reader*, edited by George Dei and Agnes Calliste. Halifax, Nova Scotia: Fernwood Publishing.

de la Torre, P., and Pesquera, B. 1994. Introduction. In *Building with our hands: New directions in Chicana studies*. Berkeley: University of California Press.

Deutsch, S. 1987. *No separate refuge: Class, culture and gender on an Anglo-Hispanic frontier in the American southwest, 1880-1940*. New York: Oxford University Press.

Dirkx, J., and Spurgin, M. 1992. Implicit theories of adult basic education teachers: How their beliefs about students shape classroom practice. *Adult Basic Education* 2(1): 20-41.

Dirlik, A. 1987. Culturalism as hegemonic ideology and liberating practice. In *Cultural Critique: The Nature and Context of Minority Discourse*, edited by A. Jan Mohamed and D. Lloyd, 6 (Spring): 13-50.

Elenes, C. A. 1997. Reclaiming the borderlands: Chicana/o identity, difference, and critical pedagogy. *Educational Theory* 47 (summer 3): 359-375.

Farr, M. 1991. *Biliteracy in the home: Practices among Mexicano families in Chicago*. Paper presented at the Biliteracy Colloquium of the Center for Applied Linguistics, January, Washington, D.C.

Feagin, J. 1991. The continuing significance of race: Antiblack discrimination in public spaces. *American Sociological Review* 56: 101-116.

Ferdman, B., Weber, R., and Ramirez, A., eds. 1994. *Literacy across languages and cultures*. New York: State University of New York Press.

Fine, M. 1989. Silencing and nurturing voice in an improbable context: Urban adolescents in public school. In *Critical pedagogy, the state, and cultural struggle*, edited by H. Giroux and P. McLaren. New York: State University of New York Press.

Flores, J., and Yudice, G. 1990. Living borders/Buscando America: Languages of Latino self-formation. *Social Text* 24, 57-84.

Foucault, M. 1972. *Power/knowledge: Selected interviews and other writings 1972-1975*, edited by C. Gordon. New York: Pantheon Books.

Fowler-Frey, J. 1996. Linguistic minority adults and literacy education. *Adult Basic Education* 6(2): 84-96.

Freire, P. 1971. *Pedagogy of the oppressed*. New York: Harper & Row.

———. 1985. *The politics of education*. Granby, Mass.: Bergin & Garvey.

Giddens, A. 1979. *Central problems in social theory: Action, structure and contradiction in social analysis*. Berkeley: University of California Press.

———. 1984. *The constitution of society: Outline of the theory of structuration*. Great Britain: Polity Press.

Giroux, H. 1983. *Theory and resistance in education: A pedagogy for the opposition*. New York: Bergin & Garvey.

Glaser, B., and Strauss, A. 1967. *The discovery of grounded theory: Strategies for qualitative research*. Chicago: Aldine Publishing.

Goetz, J., and LeCompte, M. 1984. *Ethnography and qualitative design in educational research*. New York: Academic Press.

Gonzales, R. 1972. *I am Joaquin*. New York: Bantam Pathfinders.

Gramsci, A. 1971. *Selections from the prisons notebooks*. Translated by Q. Hoare and G. Smith. New York: International Publishers.

Hall, S. 1992. New ethnicities. In *"Race," culture and difference*, edited by J. Donald and A. Rattansi. London: Sage Publications.

Hayes, E. 1989. Hispanic adults and ESL programs: Barriers to participation. *TESOL Quarterly* 23(1) 47-63.

Hill Collins, P. 1990. *Black feminist thought: Knowledge, consciousness, and the politics of empowerment*. New York: Routledge.

Horsman, J. 1990. *Something in my mind besides the everyday: Women and literacy*. Toronto, Ontario: Women's Press.

Hurtado, A. 1996. Strategic suspensions: Feminists of color theorize the production of knowledge. In *Knowledge, Difference, and Power: Essays Inspired by Women's Ways of Knowing*, edited by

Nancy Goldberger, J. Tarule, B. Clinchy, and M. Belenky. New York: Basic Books.

Hurtado, A., Gurin, P., and Peng, T. 1994. Social identities—A framework for studying the adaption of immigrants and ethnics: The adaptions of Mexican Americans in the United States. *Social Problems* 41(1): 129-151.

Jorgensen, D. 1989. *Participant observation: A methodology for human studies.* London: Sage.

Kanellos, N. 1998. *Thirty million strong: Reclaiming the Hispanic image in American culture.* Golden, Colo.: Fulcrum Publishing.

Keddie, N. 1980. Adult education: An ideology of individualism. In *Adult education for a change,* edited by J. Thompson. London: Hutchinson.

Lacapra, D., ed. 1991. *The bounds of race: Perspectives on hegemony and resistance.* New York: Cornell University Press.

Lincoln, Y., and Guba, E. 1985. *Naturalistic inquiry.* London: Sage.

Lofland, J., and Lofland, L. 1984. *Analyzing social settings: A guide to qualitative observation and analysis.* Belmont, Calif.: Wadsworth Publishers.

Lugones, M. 1990. Hablando cara a cara/Speaking face to face: An exploration of ethnocentric racism. In *Making face, making soul hacienda caras: Creative and critical perspectives by feminists of color,* edited by G. Anzaldua. San Francisco: Aunt Lute Books.

Macedo, D., and Bartolome, L. 2000. *Dancing with bigotry: Beyond the politics.* New York: St. Martin's.

Macias, R. 1990. *Latino illiteracy in the United States.* Claremont, Calif.: Claremont College, Tomas Rivera Center.

Marin, G., and Marin, B. 1989. *Research with Hispanic populations.* London: Sage.

Martin, L. 1990. Facilitating cultural diversity in adult literacy programs. In *Serving culturally diverse populations,* edited by J. Ross-Gordon, L. Martin, and D. Briscoe. San Francisco: Jossey-Bass. New Directions in Adult and Continuing Education Series 45-54.

McDonald, R. 1974. Achieving school failure: An anthropological approach to illiteracy and social stratification. In *Education and culture process: Toward an anthropology of education*, edited by G. Spindler. Austin, Tex.: Holt, Rhinehart, & Winston.

Minnich, E. 1990. *Transforming knowledge*. Philadelphia: Temple University Press.

Mirande, A. 1985. *The Chicano experience: An alternative perspective*. Notre Dame, Ind.: University of Notre Dame Press.

Montero-Sieburth, M. 1990. The education of Hispanic adults: Pedagogical strands and cultural meanings. In *Adult education in a multicultural society*, edited by B. Cassara. New York: Routledge.

Moore, M., and Stravrianos, M. 1995. Review of adult education programs and their effectiveness. A background paper for reauthorization of the Adult Education Act, Department of Education, Washington D.C.

Moraga, C., and Anzaldua, G. 1981. *This bridge called my back: Writings by radical women of color*. New York: Kitchen Table: Women of Color Press.

Mouffe, C. 1979. *Gramsci and Marxist Theory*. London: Routledge and Kegan Paul.

National Center for Education Statistics. 1993. *Adult literacy in America: A first look at the results of the national adult literacy survey*. Washington, D.C.: U.S. Government Printing Office. (Publication No. 065-000-00588-3).

National Council of La Raza. 2001. *Beyond the census: Hispanics and an American agenda*. Washington, D.C.: National Council of LaRaza.

Nieto, S. 1998. Fact or fiction: Stories of Puerto Ricans in United States schools. *Harvard Educational Review* 68(2): 133-163.

Ogbu, J. 1987. Variability in minority school performance: A problem in search of an explanation. *Anthropology and Education Quarterly* 18: 312-334.

O'Neal, S. 1986. Inhibiting midwives, usurping creators: The struggling emergence of Black women in American fiction. In *Feminist studies/Critical studies*, edited by T. De Laurentis. Indianapolis: Indiana University Press.

Pai, Y. 1990. Cultural pluralism, democracy and multicultural education. In *Adult education in a multicultural society*, edited by B.
Cassara. New York: Routledge.

Pena, D. 1998. Cultural landscapes and biodiversity: The ethnoecology
of an upper Rio Grande watershed commons. In *La gente:
Hispanio history and life in Colorado*, edited by V. C. DeBaca.
Denver: Colorado Historical Society.

Quigley, B. A. 1987. Learning to work with them: Analyzing non-par-
ticipation in adult basic education through resistance theory.
Adult Literacy and Basic Education 11(2): 63-70.

———. 1997. *Rethinking literacy education: The critical need for prac-
tice-based change.* San Francisco: Jossey Bass.

Quigley, B. A., and Holsinger, E. 1993. "Happy consciousness": Ideology and hidden curricula in literacy education. *Adult Education
Quarterly* 44(1): 17-33.

Richardson, C. 1980. Minority adult participation in ABE programs:
Cultural vs. structural factors. *Ethnic Groups: An International
Periodical of Ethnic Studies* 2(4): 307-326.

Rockhill, K. 1983. Motivation out of context. *Mobius* 3: 21-27.

Scanlan, C., and Darkenwald, G. 1984. Identifying deterrents to participation in continuing education. *Adult Education Quarterly*
34(3):155-166.

Scott, J. 1990. *Domination and the arts of resistance: Hidden transcripts.*
New Haven, Conn.: Yale University Press.

Segura, D. 1993. Slipping through the cracks: Dilemmas in Chicana
education. In *Building with our hands: New directions in Chicana
studies*, edited by A. de la Torre and B. Pesquera. Berkeley: University of California Press.

Seidman, I. 1991. *Interviewing as qualitative research: A guide for re-
searchers in education and the social sciences.* New York: Teachers
College Press.

Shorris, E. 1992. *Latinos: A biography of the people.* New York: W.W.
Norton & Co.

Sibley, G. 1992. Colonization and its consequences-Part I. *The Head-
waters Trib* 2(3): 1-2,6.

Sparks, B. 1993. The politics of Latino culture in adult basic education: Negotiating identity. Paper presented at the annual meeting of the American Association of Adult and Continuing Education, Dallas, November 1993.

————. 1995. The impact of structural-cultural factors on nonparticipation in adult basic education by Chicano/a adults in urban communities in Colorado. Ed.D. diss., University of Wisconsin-Milwaukee, May 1995. Abstract in *Dissertation Abstracts International* 56, A1627.

————. 1998. Repeat performance: How adult education reproduces the status quo. *Journal of Adult Education* 26(1): 3-15.

Sparks, B., and MacDaniels, C. 1999. Subjectivity in women's learning: A case for participatory inquiry. ERIC Clearinghouse for Adult, Career, and Vocational Education, ED42820.

Sparks, B., and Peterson, E. 2000. Adult basic education and the crisis of accountability. In *Handbook of Adult and Continuing Education*, edited by Arthur Wilson and Elizabeth Hayes. San Francisco: Jossey Bass.

Stake, R. 1994. Case studies. In *Handbook of qualitative research*, edited by N. Denzin & Y. Lincoln. San Francisco: Sage.

Stanfield II, J. 1993. Methodological reflections: An introduction. In *Race and ethnicity in research methods*, edited by J. Stanfield II and R. Dennis. New York: Sage Publications.

Stavans, I. 1995 . *The Hispanic condition: Reflections on culture and identity in America*. New York: Harper Perennial.

Stuckey, J. E. 1991. *The violence of literacy*. Portsmouth, N.H.: Boynton/Cook Publishers.

Takaki, R. 1993. *A different mirror: A history of multicultural America*. Boston: Little, Brown & Co.

Torres, C. A. 1990. *The politics of nonformal education in Latin America*. New York: Praeger.

Tumulty, K. 2001. Courting a sleeping giant. *Time Magazine*, 11 June.

U.S. Bureau of the Census. 2000. *Colorado Quick Facts*. Available from http://Quickfacts.census.gov/gfd/states/08000.html.

U.S. Department of Education. 1998. *State-administered adult education program 1998 enrollment of participants by race/ethnicity.* Available at www.ed.gov/offices/OVAE/98ethnic.html, Office of Vocational and Adult Education, Division of Adult Education and Literacy.

U.S. Senate. 1995. Committee on Labor and Human Relations. *Adult Education and Family Literacy Reform Act. Hearing before the Subcommittee on Education, Arts, and Humanities.* 104th Cong. 1st sess. 19 May.

Valdes, G. 1993. Bilingualism: Testing, a special case of bias. In *Hispanics: National interests, group interests, and public policy,* edited by W. Van Horn. Colloquium on Ethnicity and public policy, University of Wisconsin System Institute on Race and Ethnicity, Green Bay, Wisc.

Vallejo, M. E. 1998. Recollections of the Colorado coal strike, 1913-1914. In *La gente:Hispanio history and life in Colorado,* edited by V.C. DeBaca. Denver: Colorado Historical Society.

Vogel Zanger, V. 1994. "Not joined in": The social context of English literacy development for Hispanic youth. In *Literacy across languages and cultures,* edited by B. Federman, R. Weber, & A. Ramirez. New York: University of New York Press.

Walsh, C. 1991. *Pedagogy and the struggle for voice: Issues of language, power and schooling for Puerto Ricans.* New York: Bergin & Garvey.

Weiler, K. 1988. *Women teaching for change: Gender, class and power.* New York: Bergin & Garvey.

Weiss, L. 1983. Schooling and cultural production: A comparison of Black and White lived culture. In *Ideology and practice in schooling,* edited by M. Apple & L. Weiss. Philadelphia: Temple University Press.

Westcott, M. 1983. Women's studies as a strategy for change: Between criticism and vision. In *Modern feminisms: Political, literary, cultural,* edited by M. Humm. New York: Columbia University Press.

Williams, R. 1981. *Culture.* Great Britian: Fontana Press.

Willis, P. 1977. *Learning to labor: How working class kids get working class jobs.* New York: Columbia University Press.